DEBRETT'S

A Modern & Royal Marriage

PRINCE WILLIAM OF WALES

CATHERINE MIDDLETON

FOREWORD BY JULIAN FELLOWES

First published in Great Britain in 2011
by Simon & Schuster UK Ltd
A CBS COMPANY

1 3 5 7 9 10 8 6 4 2

SIMON & SCHUSTER ILLUSTRATED BOOKS
Simon & Schuster UK Ltd
222 Gray's Inn Road
London
WC1X 8HB

www.simonandschuster.co.uk

Simon & Schuster Australia, Sydney
Simon & Schuster India, New Delhi

A CIP catalogue copy for this book is available
from the British Library

ISBN: 978-0-85720-685-5

Printed and bound in Spain

DEBRETT'S

MANAGING EDITOR
Elizabeth Wyse

DESIGNER
Karen Wilks

TEXT
Charles Kidd
Rowan Pelling
Elizabeth Wyse

PICTURE RESEARCH
Sheila Lee

INDEX
Christine Shaw

CHAIRMAN Conrad Free
COMMERCIAL DIRECTOR David Miller

www.debretts.com

A Modern

Royal

Marriage

PRINCE WILLIAM OF WALES

&

CATHERINE MIDDLETON

Contents

29 April 2011

*"Now know ye that we have consented and
do by these presents signify our consent to the
contracting of matrimony between our most dearly
beloved grandson Prince William Arthur Philip
Louis of Wales, K.G., and our trusty and well-
beloved Catherine Elizabeth Middleton."*

Foreword

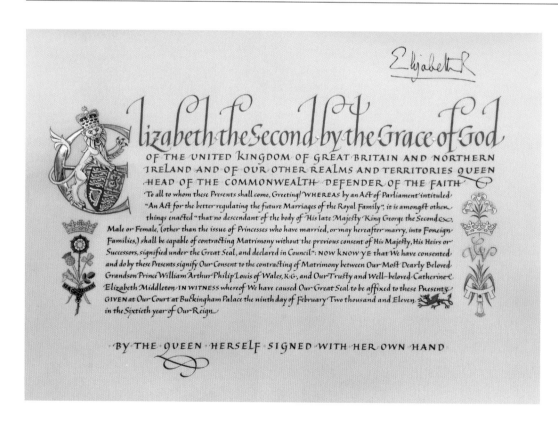

Under the 1772 Royal Marriages Act, Prince William was required to ask his grandmother's permission to marry. The beautifully illuminated Instrument of Consent was sent to the couple after their marriage. Three floral emblems, the thistle, shamrock and rose, represent the United Kingdom. The white lily is a reference to the feast day of Catherine of Siena (29 April).

It is, I think, safe to say that we expect the royal family to live their lives as a larger and more fascinating version of our own. And if, these days, we will concede them some privacy, nevertheless their great events must be public, glittering models of our own great events, recognisable in every detail and somehow as interesting to us as if we knew them well. Which of course, in a way, we do. Walter Bagehot described the marriage of the future King Edward VII, as "the brilliant edition of a universal fact", and his point can seldom have been better illustrated than by the wedding on 29 April 2011, of His Royal Highness Prince William of Wales and Miss Catherine Middleton.

Was it a surprise to us, to find that the loyalty of the British people to their royal house remains so fervent? I suspect so. And while fashionable republicans are no doubt fainting in coils of disappointment north of the park at the thought of all that ritual still to come, those christenings, those processions, those jubilees, most of us take comfort in the unarguable truth that there remains one institution that can unify us in our enthusiasm, unify us, in fact, in a kind of love. Whenever we are given a chance to demonstrate that love, it serves as a timely reminder that we are still a nation.

Of course much has been written about Miss Middleton's roots and the departure from our traditions that she represents, but this overlooks the main tradition of the British monarchy, which is constantly to reinvent itself, in order to keep in step with the people of these islands. In the Middle Ages, marriage to English heiresses was deemed useful (which it no doubt was), until they gave way to the daughters of Kings, of France and Spain and Portugal and Denmark, who all too often led to uneasy alliances. Next came a hundred and fifty years' worth of wives and husbands from minor German duchies and principalities, the majority royal enough to marry but not so royal as to risk participation in an unwanted conflict.

Then a big change arrives in 1917, when King George and Queen Mary decide that, in future the obligation to marry royal will go and their children may seek partners among the British peerage. This was a far greater departure from tradition than anything since. At the time, the relaxation of the rules was denounced as fatal to the monarchy. In fact, the new code gave us the late Queen Elizabeth, the Queen Mother, one of the most popular queen consorts we have ever known. Similarly, Diana, Princess of Wales, bred in a like stable, achieved an iconic status, far beyond anything those no doubt dutiful but seldom charismatic princesses from Mecklenberg or Brunswick or Saxe-Meiningen, ever came close to.

Now we have Miss Middleton, transmogrified into Her Royal Highness The Duchess of Cambridge, who embodies, in her person and her family, the values that today's society holds dear. Their story is a tale of hard work rewarded, of strong family values, of sensible thinking with the blessing of good looks, all riches to be added to the treasure trove of the family she has joined, to help the young Prince and Princess steer this ancient institution into the new age.

In *A Modern Royal Marriage*, Debrett's has given us all a fitting and lasting memento of a very happy day, with all the pomp and pageantry that we do so well, as well as reminders of the quiet and personal moments that made this modern royal marriage so memorable. I hope you will cherish it as a reminder that we can still feel proud to be British. In fact, it was hard not to sense that, on that special wedding day, we plighted our troth with the young couple, as they did with each other and, like all those men and women cheering down The Mall, I wish them and us every happiness in each other's company, during the years ahead.

JULIAN FELLOWES

the ROYAL OAK

VICTORIA REGINA 1837-1887.

Genealogy

The genealogical aspects of this royal marriage are highly original. Prince William's antecedents are well known, but Catherine Middleton's ancestry is intriguing. Through Sarah Fairfax, a mid-17th century ancestress who came from a Yorkshire land-owning family, Catherine is descended from the Earls of Northumberland and thereby from Elizabeth Mortimer, a great-grand-daughter of King Edward III. So, although Catherine is not actually from an aristocratic family she does, in fact, have royal blood.

The Royal Family Tree

This pedigree shows the descendants of King George VI, being the immediate members of the present royal family. The first nineteen in line to the throne are named, starting with the Prince of Wales and ending with Arthur Chatto. The many post-nominal letters signifying the orders of chivalry borne by members of the royal family have been omitted on this family tree for the sake of simplicity.

KING GEORGE VI = LADY ELIZABETH BOWES-LYON
(1895-1952)   (1900-2002)
Emperor of India   *da of 14th Earl of Strathmore and Kinghorne*

PRINCE PHILIP = QUEEN ELIZABETH II
(b 1921)   (b 1926)
Duke of Edinburgh   *Married 1947*

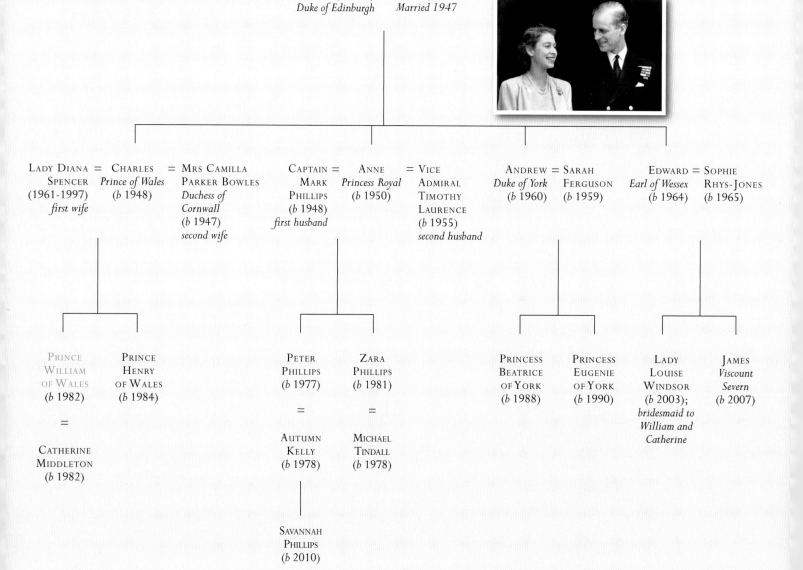

LADY DIANA = CHARLES = MRS CAMILLA   CAPTAIN = ANNE = VICE   ANDREW = SARAH   EDWARD = SOPHIE
SPENCER *Prince of Wales* PARKER BOWLES   MARK *Princess Royal* ADMIRAL   *Duke of York* FERGUSON   *Earl of Wessex* RHYS-JONES
(1961-1997) (b 1948) *Duchess of*   PHILLIPS (b 1950) TIMOTHY   (b 1960) (b 1959)   (b 1964) (b 1965)
first wife   *Cornwall*   (b 1948)   LAURENCE
    (b 1947)   *first husband*   (b 1955)
    second wife   *second husband*

PRINCE   PRINCE   PETER   ZARA   PRINCESS   PRINCESS   LADY   JAMES
WILLIAM   HENRY   PHILLIPS   PHILLIPS   BEATRICE   EUGENIE   LOUISE   *Viscount*
OF WALES   OF WALES   (b 1977)   (b 1981)   OF YORK   OF YORK   WINDSOR   *Severn*
(b 1982)   (b 1984)   (b 1988)   (b 1990)   (b 2003);   (b 2007)
        =   =   *bridesmaid to*
=   *William and*
        AUTUMN   MICHAEL   *Catherine*
CATHERINE   KELLY   TINDALL
MIDDLETON   (b 1978)   (b 1978)
(b 1982)

SAVANNAH
PHILLIPS
(b 2010)

ANTONY ARMSTRONG-JONES = PRINCESS MARGARET
Earl of Snowdon (1930-2002)
(*b* 1930) *Married 1960*

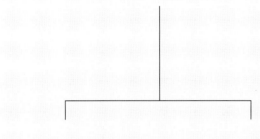

DAVID = LADY SERENA
ARMSTRONG-JONES STANHOPE
Viscount Linley (*b* 1970)
(*b* 1961)

LADY SARAH = DANIEL
ARMSTRONG-JONES CHATTO
(*b* 1964) (*b* 1957)

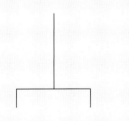

HON. CHARLES ARMSTRONG-JONES (*b* 1999)

HON. MARGARITA ARMSTRONG-JONES (*b* 2002); *bridesmaid to William and Catherine*

SAMUEL CHATTO (*b* 1996)

ARTHUR CHATTO (*b* 1999)

SUCCESSION TO THE THRONE

The succession to the British throne is governed by common law and by statute. The succession follows male-preference primogeniture, in other words a male heir takes precedence over his older female sibling. Unlike the former French monarchy, however, Britain's laws of succession never included the Salic law, whereby a female heir was excluded from acceding to the throne, and which disallowed any claim to the throne through a female heir. Indeed, some of our greatest monarchs have been female: Queen Elizabeth I, Queen Victoria and our present Sovereign, Queen Elizabeth II. It will be interesting to see whether, in the generation following William and Catherine, the laws of succession are amended to treat male and female heirs as equal, with primogeniture the exclusive right to succession.

THE PRINCE OF WALES

THE DUKE OF CAMBRIDGE

PRINCE HENRY OF WALES

THE DUKE OF YORK

PRINCESS BEATRICE OF YORK

PRINCESS EUGENIE OF YORK

THE EARL OF WESSEX

VISCOUNT SEVERN

LADY LOUISE WINDSOR

THE PRINCESS ROYAL

PETER PHILLIPS

SAVANNAH PHILLIPS

ZARA PHILLIPS

VISCOUNT LINLEY

THE HON CHARLES ARMSTRONG-JONES

THE HON MARGARITA ARMSTRONG-JONES

LADY SARAH CHATTO

SAMUEL CHATTO

ARTHUR CHATTO

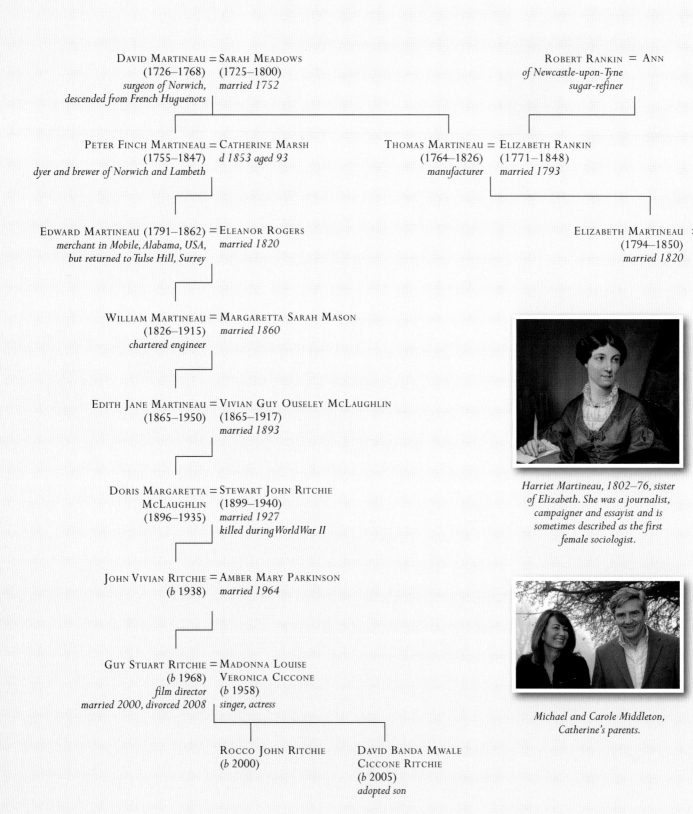

David Martineau = Sarah Meadows
(1726–1768)   (1725–1800)
surgeon of Norwich,   *married 1752*
descended from French Huguenots

Robert Rankin = Ann
of Newcastle-upon-Tyne
sugar-refiner

Peter Finch Martineau = Catherine Marsh
(1755–1847)   *d 1853 aged 93*
dyer and brewer of Norwich and Lambeth

Thomas Martineau = Elizabeth Rankin
(1764–1826)   (1771–1848)
manufacturer   *married 1793*

Edward Martineau (1791–1862) = Eleanor Rogers
merchant in Mobile, Alabama, USA,   *married 1820*
but returned to Tulse Hill, Surrey

Elizabeth Martineau
(1794–1850)
married 1820

William Martineau = Margaretta Sarah Mason
(1826–1915)   *married 1860*
chartered engineer

Edith Jane Martineau = Vivian Guy Ouseley McLaughlin
(1865–1950)   (1865–1917)
married 1893

Harriet Martineau, 1802–76, sister of Elizabeth. She was a journalist, campaigner and essayist and is sometimes described as the first female sociologist.

Doris Margaretta = Stewart John Ritchie
McLaughlin   (1899–1940)
(1896–1935)   *married 1927*
killed during World War II

John Vivian Ritchie = Amber Mary Parkinson
(b 1938)   *married 1964*

Guy Stuart Ritchie = Madonna Louise
(b 1968)   Veronica Ciccone
film director   (b 1958)
married 2000, divorced 2008   *singer, actress*

Michael and Carole Middleton, Catherine's parents.

Rocco John Ritchie
(b 2000)

David Banda Mwale
Ciccone Ritchie
(b 2005)
adopted son

Catherine Middleton's family tree represents an interesting mixture of professions and trades. There are surgeons, clergymen and lawyers, merchants and textile manufacturers, carpenters, builders and labourers. Her ancestry covers a wide section of the country, with strong influences from Leeds, North Yorkshire and County Durham. Catherine can claim to be 'an English rose', for she is almost entirely of English blood. Perhaps her most exotic ancestry comes from the French Huguenot family of Martineau, through whom Catherine is a sixth cousin once removed of the film director, Guy Ritchie.

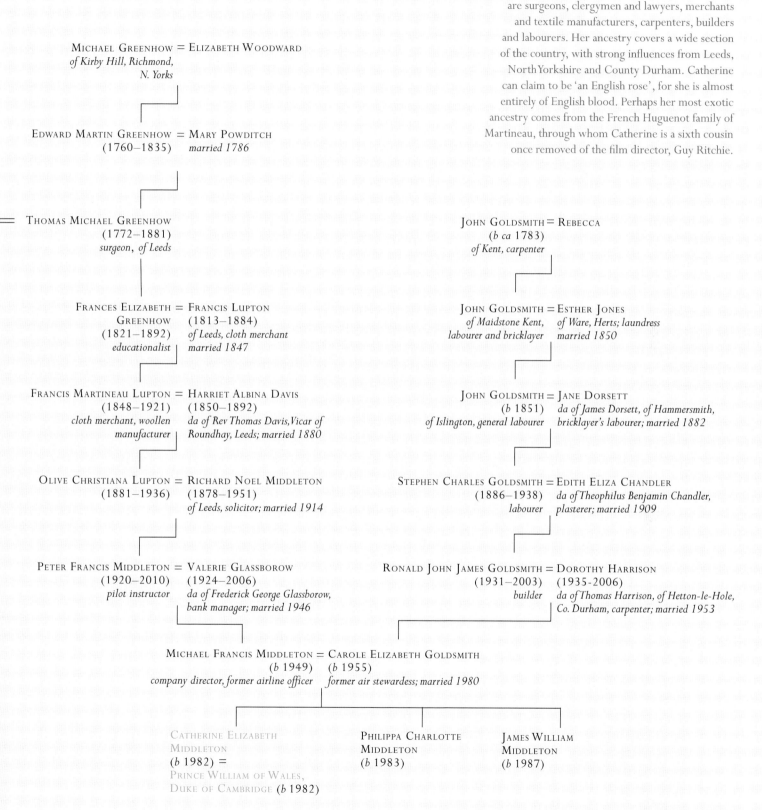

MICHAEL GREENHOW = ELIZABETH WOODWARD
of Kirby Hill, Richmond,
N. Yorks

EDWARD MARTIN GREENHOW = MARY POWDITCH
(1760–1835)   *married 1786*

THOMAS MICHAEL GREENHOW
(1772–1881)
surgeon, of Leeds

JOHN GOLDSMITH = REBECCA
(*b ca* 1783)
of Kent, carpenter

FRANCES ELIZABETH = FRANCIS LUPTON
GREENHOW   (1813–1884)
(1821–1892)   *of Leeds, cloth merchant*
educationalist   *married 1847*

JOHN GOLDSMITH = ESTHER JONES
of Maidstone Kent,   *of Ware, Herts; laundress*
labourer and bricklayer *married 1850*

FRANCIS MARTINEAU LUPTON = HARRIET ALBINA DAVIS
(1848–1921)   (1850–1892)
cloth merchant, woollen *da of Rev Thomas Davis, Vicar of*
manufacturer   *Roundhay, Leeds; married 1880*

JOHN GOLDSMITH = JANE DORSETT
(*b* 1851)   *da of James Dorsett, of Hammersmith,*
of Islington, general labourer *bricklayer's labourer; married 1882*

OLIVE CHRISTIANA LUPTON = RICHARD NOEL MIDDLETON
(1881–1936)   (1878–1951)
                        of Leeds, solicitor; married 1914

STEPHEN CHARLES GOLDSMITH = EDITH ELIZA CHANDLER
(1886–1938)   *da of Theophilus Benjamin Chandler,*
labourer   *plasterer; married 1909*

PETER FRANCIS MIDDLETON = VALERIE GLASSBOROW
(1920–2010)   (1924–2006)
pilot instructor   *da of Frederick George Glassborow,*
                        bank manager; married 1946

RONALD JOHN JAMES GOLDSMITH = DOROTHY HARRISON
(1931–2003)   (1935-2006)
builder   *da of Thomas Harrison, of Hetton-le-Hole,*
                            Co. Durham, carpenter; married 1953

MICHAEL FRANCIS MIDDLETON = CAROLE ELIZABETH GOLDSMITH
(*b* 1949)   (*b* 1955)
company director, former airline officer *former air stewardess; married 1980*

CATHERINE ELIZABETH
MIDDLETON
(*b* 1982) =
PRINCE WILLIAM OF WALES,
DUKE OF CAMBRIDGE (*b* 1982)

PHILIPPA CHARLOTTE
MIDDLETON
(*b* 1983)

JAMES WILLIAM
MIDDLETON
(*b* 1987)

How They Are Related

William and Kate are 14th cousins once removed

Sir Thomas Fairfax (*d* 1521)
Yorkshire landowner

Sir Nicholas Fairfax (*d* 1570) = Jane Palmes
of Walton and Gilling Castle, Yorks   *da of Guy Palmes, of Lindley, Yorks,*
Sergeant-at-Law to King Henry VII

Margaret Fairfax = Sir William Belasyse (*d* 1604 *aged 81*)
of Newborough, Yorks

Sir Henry Belasyse, 1st Bt (1555—1624) = Ursula Fairfax (*d* 1633)
MP for Thirsk   *da of Sir Thomas Fairfax, of Denton, Yorks*

Thomas Belasyse, 1st Viscount Fauconberg (1577—1653) = Barbara Cholmeley (*d* 1619)
Fought for King Charles I at Marston Moor   *da of Sir Henry Cholmeley, of Whitby*

John Belasyse, 1st Baron Belasyse (1614—1689) = Lady Anne Paulet (*d* 1694)
MP for Thirsk; Royalist soldier   *da of 5th Marquess of Winchester*
Fought at battles of Edgehill, Newbury and Naseby

Barbara Belasyse (*d* 1740) = Sir John Webb (*d* 1745, *Aix-le-Chapelle, France*)
co-heiress   *3rd Bt, of Hatherop, Glos and of Odstock, Wilts*

Mary Webb (*d* in childbirth 1719) = James, 1st Earl Waldegrave (1684—1741)
Ambassador to Vienna and Paris

James, 2nd Earl Waldegrave (1715—1763) = Maria Walpole
d of smallpox   *A famous beauty painted by Gainsborough and Reynolds;*
illegitimate da of Sir Edward Walpole by Dorothy,
da of Hammond Clement, postmaster at Darlington

Lady Anne Horatia Waldegrave (*d* 1801) = Admiral Lord Hugh Seymour (1759—1801)
5th son of 2nd Marquess of Hertford

Col Sir Horace Beauchamp Seymour (1791—1851) = Elizabeth Palk (*d* 1827)
MP for Lisburn, Antrim, Oxford, Bodmin and Midhurst   *da of Sir Lawrence Palk, 2nd Bt*

Adelaide Seymour (1825—1877) = 4th Earl Spencer, KG, PC (1798—1857)
Lord Chamberlain HM Household 1846—48
Lord Steward HM Household 1854—1857

6th Earl Spencer, KG, GCVO (1857—1922) = Hon Margaret Baring (1868—1906)
Lord Lieutenant Northamptonshire, Lord Chamberlain 1905—12   *da of 1st Baron Revelstoke, Director of Bank of England 1879—91*

7th Earl Spencer (1892—1975) = Lady Cynthia Hamilton, DCVO
Served WWI (wounded)   *Lady of the Bedchamber to Queen Elizabeth the Queen Mother,*
Lord Lieutenant Northamptonshire 1952—67   *da of 3rd Duke of Abercorn*

8th Earl Spencer (1924—1992) = Hon Frances Burke Roche (1936—2004)
Served WWII (despatches)   *later Mrs Shand Kydd, da of 4th Baron Fermoy*
Equerry to King George VI 1950—1952 and
to Queen Elizabeth II 1952—54

Lady Diana Spencer (1961—1997) = Charles Prince of Wales, KG, KT, OM, PC (*b* 1948)

Prince William of Wales, KG (*b* 1982),
Duke of Cambridge

AGNES GASCOIGNE
da of Sir William Gascoigne, of Gawthorpe, Yorks

Prince William and Catherine Middleton are very distantly related – they are fourteenth cousins once removed (the 'removed' simply means that there is a difference of one generation in their descent from Sir Thomas Fairfax). The Fairfax family were prominent landowners in North Yorkshire in the 16th and 17th centuries. Some members of the family were Royalists, others were Parliamentarians. William's descent from Sir Thomas Fairfax is through his mother, Diana Princess of Wales, whereas Catherine's descent is through her father, Michael Middleton.

WILLIAM FAIRFAX (*d* 1588) = (1) ANNE BAKER
May have migrated from Yorkshire to Suffolk as a result of the flourishing wool trade in that county; buried at Walsingham, Norfolk   (2) KATE TANFIELD

JOHN FAIRFAX (*d* 1614) = MARY BIRCH
Master of the Great Hospital, Norwich   *da of John Birch, of Norwich*

REV'D BENJAMIN FAIRFAX (1592–1675) = SARAH GALLIARD
of Rumburgh, Suffolk   *da of Roger Galliard,*
In Holy Orders until ejected 1662 upon Act of Uniformity   *of Ashwell Thorpe, Norfolk*

BENJAMIN FAIRFAX (*d* 1708) = BRIDGET STRINGER (*d* 1669)
of Halesworth, Suffolk   *da of Walter Stringer, of Chester*

SARAH FAIRFAX (1654–1687) = REV'D JOHN MEADOWS (1622–1697)
  non-conformist Vicar of Ousden (ejected 1662 upon Act of Uniformity)

PHILIP MEADOWS (1679–1752) = MARGARET HALL (1691–1765)
Mayor of Norwich 1734   *of Norwich*

SARAH MEADOWS (1725–1800) = DAVID MARTINEAU (1726–1768)
  Surgeon

THOMAS MARTINEAU (1764–1826) = ELIZABETH RANKIN (1771–1848)
Manufacturer of camelots and bombazine

ELIZABETH MARTINEAU (1794–1850) = THOS M. GREENHOW (1792–1881)
Sister of Harriet Martineau, the political journalist   *Surgeon and sanitary reformer of Leeds*

FRANCES GREENHOW (1821–1892) = FRANCIS LUPTON (1813–1884)
Educationalist   *Cloth merchant of Leeds*

FRANCIS LUPTON (1848–1921) = HARRIET DAVIS (1850–1892)
Cloth merchant and woollen manufacturer

OLIVE LUPTON (1881–1936) = NOEL MIDDLETON (1878–1951)
  Solicitor, Leeds

PETER FRANCIS MIDDLETON (1920–2010) = VALERIE GLASSBOROW (1924–2006)
Pilot instructor

MICHAEL MIDDLETON (*b* 1949) = CAROLE GOLDSMITH (*b* 1955)
Director of 'Party Pieces'

CATHERINE MIDDLETON (*b* 1982),
DUCHESS OF CAMBRIDGE

Elizabeth Woodville,
wife of King Edward IV

"I have found it impossible to carry the heavy burden of responsibility and to discharge my duties as king as I would wish to do without the help and support of the woman I love."
King Edward VIII's abdication speech

Commoners in the Royal Family

THE TERM COMMONER is divisive and widely disputed. Some authorities argue that it applies to someone who is neither the sovereign nor a peer. But this narrow definition would exclude members of the royal family, such as Princess Anne and Prince Harry, who are not peers. According to this definition, both Lady Elizabeth Bowes-Lyon and Lady Diana Spencer would have been 'commoners' until they married their respective husbands, although this would hardly conform to the general understanding of the word.

Although the great majority of queen consorts in our royal line of succession have been princesses from other European ruling houses, there are several spouses that stand out by being of a more 'home-grown' variety. The first of such queens is Elizabeth Woodville, wife of King Edward IV.

Elizabeth Woodville (*top left*) was the eldest daughter of a mere knight, Sir Richard Woodville (later ennobled as Earl Rivers). Elizabeth's secret marriage to King Edward IV on 1 May 1464 enraged Edward's cousin and chief supporter, Warwick 'the Kingmaker', who had been attempting to engineer a marriage between Edward and a French princess. Nevertheless Elizabeth Woodville became queen consort, and her many brothers and sisters were married into some of the most powerful families of the nobility. Elizabeth Woodville's eldest daughter, Elizabeth of York, married King Henry VII, an alliance that greatly bolstered his claim to the throne. All these three are ancestors of the present royal family.

Four of King Henry VIII's six wives would perhaps be thought of as 'commoners'. These are Anne Boleyn, Jane Seymour, Catherine Howard and Catherine Parr. All these wives, however, came from semi-aristocratic families, particularly Anne Boleyn (*left*) and Catherine Howard (first cousins) who were both nieces of Thomas Howard, 3rd Duke of Norfolk. Their aristocratic blood spared neither of them the executioner's axe.

The next 'home-grown' consort (although never queen consort) was Anne Hyde, wife to James Duke of York, who died in 1671, 14 years before her husband ascended the throne. Anne Hyde was the eldest daughter of Edward Hyde, 1st Earl of Clarendon, Lord High Chancellor of England. Her only surviving children became queens regnant, Queen Mary II and Queen Anne, but died without leaving surviving issue.

In 1772, King George III passed the Royal Marriages Act, which provided that no descendant of King George II under the age of 25 (with the exception of princesses married into foreign families) might contract matrimony without first obtaining the consent of the Sovereign in Council. Over the age of 25, notice of an intention to marry was to be given to the Privy Council.

When George Prince of Wales (later King George IV) came of age in 1783 he fell violently in love with a respectable Roman Catholic widow of 27, Mrs Fitzherbert. George's passion for her knew no bounds, but the only way he could get her was by marriage. On 21 December 1785 a marriage ceremony was performed in Mrs Fitzherbert's London house. The marriage was null and void; even if the marriage had not contravened the terms of the Royal Marriages Act, George, as the husband of a Roman Catholic, would have lost his position as heir to the throne under the terms of the Act of Settlement.

Edward (later Edward VIII), first met Mrs Simpson, American, once divorced and since re-married, whilst he was still Prince of Wales. By the time he succeeded to the throne, on 20 January 1936, he was besotted with her and was determined to marry her, despite the fact that he was sovereign head of the Church of England and she was already divorced and estranged from her second husband. The government refused to countenance such a marriage and, after nearly 11 months, Edward abdicated in favour of his brother.

Once Wallis's divorce from Ernest Simpson became final she and the former king were married in France. In March 1937 Edward had been created Duke of Windsor by the new king, George VI, and in May he received 'reconferment' of the qualification of Royal Highness. This style was reserved to him alone and could not extend to his wife.

Catherine and William will follow in the footsteps of a succession of monarchs with the same name and diverse fortunes. Their forebears include a Norman conqueror, a flighty young woman who was beheaded for her infidelity, a champion of Protestantism who wrested the crown from a Catholic king and a religious and stoic queen whose failure to produce a son precipitated the English Reformation.

Four King Williams

Duke William of Normandy (d. 1087, in Caen), known as William the Conqueror, was born in 1027 or 1028, the illegitimate son of Duke Robert of Normandy, a nominal vassal of the King of France. He went to England in 1051 to visit his first cousin once removed, King Edward the Confessor, who was childless and who nominated William as his successor. When he died, however, his brother-in-law, Earl Harold of Wessex, was chosen as his successor and crowned at Westminster Abbey. William at once began careful preparations for an invasion, and the fate of England was decided at the Battle of Hastings, 14 October 1066, when, after a day's fighting, Harold was killed by an arrow piercing his eye.

William was crowned on Christmas Day 1066, and proved an able administrator. Gradually English lords were superseded by Norman and other French barons, the Continental system of feudal land tenure was introduced and the Church was reformed.

William II (William Rufus) was William the Conqueror's third son. His older brother Robert ('Curthose'), Duke of Normandy, had rebelled against his father. Nevertheless the Conqueror left his Norman duchy to Robert and his English kingdom to William.

William alternated between supporting his brother against the King of France, and opposing him for the control of the duchy. In 1096 Robert joined the First Crusade and resigned Normandy to William for 10,000 marks.

William II never married and his rapacity made him deeply unpopular in England. He helped himself to Church revenues, and the Church Chronicles implied he was homosexual. He died in 1100 while hunting in the New Forest, shot by an 'accidental' arrow fired by his knight companion. No-one was ever held to account for his death and he was buried with scant ceremony, denied religious rites, in Winchester Cathedral.

William III, born 1650, was the son of Mary, the eldest daughter of King Charles I, and the Prince of Orange. He was educated at Leyden, eventually becoming Captain General of the Dutch Forces and Stadhouder (Provincial Governor) of the United Provinces of the Netherlands.

William's uncle King Charles II had no legitimate children and his heir to the English throne was his brother, James, then Duke of York. William married Mary, James's daughter, in 1677. They had no children.

James was crowned in 1685, but his determination to bring the country back to Catholicism was a disaster. William seized his chance, landing at Brixham in 1688, intent on ensuring the Protestant interest. He gathered many supporters on his march to London and James fled to France. William and Mary were crowned joint sovereigns in April 1689. Mary died of smallpox in 1692 and William ruled alone for the rest of his life, an austere and unloved monarch. He died, after a fall from a horse, in 1702.

William IV was born in 1765, the third son of King George III and Queen Charlotte. With little chance of ever ascending the throne he went to sea at the age of 14, though his naval career was undistinguished.

In 1789 King George III created William Duke of Clarence and in 1811 Admiral of the Fleet. William enjoyed a long-standing liaison with the comedy actress, Mrs Jordan, with whom he had ten children.

With the death of Princess Charlotte, the Prince Regent's daughter, in childbirth, there was a scramble for the sons of George III to beget legitimate heirs. William's marriage to Adelaide of Saxe-Meiningen took place in 1818, but the union was childless.

The Prince Regent ruled, as George IV, from 1820–30. He had been predeceased by his next brother, so William succeeded to the throne, following a modest coronation, and ruled for seven years. His rule was beset by political unrest, but he was respected as a man who held his country's interests at heart.

"My tribulations are so great, my life so disturbed by the plans daily invented to further the king's wicked intention, the surprises which the king gives me, with certain persons of his council, are so mortal, and my treatment is what God knows, that it is enough to shorten ten lives, much more mine."
Queen Catherine of Aragon

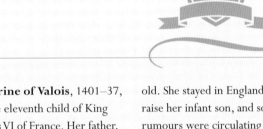

Five Queen Catherines

Catherine of Valois, 1401–37, was the eleventh child of King Charles VI of France. Her father, known as 'Charles the Mad', suffered from porphyria, the 'royal malady', which afflicted many of Charles's descendants, most notably King Henry VI and King George III.

In 1420, Catherine married Henry V, the last great warrior king of the Middle Ages, who renewed the English campaign for the crown of France, and is celebrated for his great victory at the Battle of Agincourt in 1415. The marriage between Catherine and Henry produced only one child, a son, the future King Henry VI, last of the House of Lancaster.

Henry V died in 1422, when Catherine was only 21 years old. She stayed in England to raise her infant son, and soon rumours were circulating of an intrigue between the queen and Edmund Beaufort, the 19-year-old grandson of John of Gaunt. A statute was hurriedly passed in the 1427–28 parliamentary session forbidding the queen to re-marry.

Some four years later Catherine married her handsome Welsh servant Owen Tudor and the marriage was accepted as legal by the King's Council. The eldest of Catherine and Owen's three sons, Edmund, married the 13-year old orphan, Lady Margaret Beaufort, heiress of the line of John of Gaunt, Duke of Lancaster, and from this marriage sprang King Henry VII and the House of Tudor.

Catherine of Aragon (1485–1536) was the daughter of King Ferdinand of Aragon and Queen Isabella of Castile. Her first husband, Henry VIII's older brother Arthur, died just five months after the wedding. She married his glamorous, vibrant brother, but failed to provide the male heir he so desperately desired. She endured the annulment of her marriage, and her supplanting by Anne Boleyn, but kept her head.

Catherine Howard, the fifth wife of King Henry VIII, was the niece of the 3rd Duke of Norfolk. Promiscuous and headstrong, she was already indulging in torrid affairs from the age of 14. When her uncle introduced her to 50-year-old Henry he was bewitched, and the pair were married in 1540. Catherine resumed an affair with a previous lover and when Henry learnt of her betrayal his lust turned to hatred. She was beheaded on 13 February 1542.

Catherine Parr (1512–48) was already twice widowed when she fell in love with the dashing, but unstable, Thomas Seymour. Fate intervened, however, and she became the last wife of Henry VIII in 1543. Childless, she was a discreet and affectionate step-mother to his three children. When Henry died in 1547, Catherine married her former suitor, but died soon after giving birth to a daughter.

Catherine of Braganza (1638–1705) was the daughter of King John IV of Portugal. Bringing a substantial dowry of £300,000, with the naval bases of Tangier and Bombay thrown in, she married the restored, but impoverished, King Charles II of England in 1662. Samuel Pepys reported in his diary on seeing her for the first time, 'though she be not very charming, yet she hath a good, modest and innocent look, which is pleasing.'

Charles's grief at Catherine's inability to bear a surviving child was tempered by his genuine fondness for his wife. She maintained a dignified attitude of forbearance to Charles's mistresses and showed many acts of kindness to his illegitimate children.

After Charles died in 1685 Catherine lived at Somerset House. She stayed in London after her brother-in-law King James II fled the country in 1688, but did not get along with his successors, William and Mary, and returned to Portugal, living there for the last 12 years of her life.

A Historical View

Over the last century royal weddings have evolved from muted, semi-private affairs to eagerly anticipated state occasions, watched worldwide, minutely dissected and discussed. Queen Victoria may have chosen the semi-privacy of St. James's Palace, but crowds were fascinated by a genuine royal romance and her white wedding dress set the standard for Victorian brides. Today we would find the media and public frenzy surrounding Princess Elizabeth's wedding dress wholly familiar.

"I wore a white satin dress, with a deep flounce of Honiton lace, an imitation of an old design. My jewels were my Turkish diamond necklace & earrings & dear Albert's beautiful sapphire brooch."
Queen Victoria's Journal

The Wedding of Queen Victoria

THE MARRIAGE OF Queen Victoria and her first cousin, Prince Albert of Saxe-Coburg and Gotha, was the first wedding of a reigning queen since Queen Mary married in 1554. Queen Victoria was quite lovestruck, describing the prince as possessing "such beautiful blue eyes, and exquisite nose, and such a pretty mouth with delicate moustachios and slight but very slight whiskers". As reigning Queen she proposed to Albert and was accepted. The wedding was held on 10 February 1840 in the royal chapel of St. James's Palace, London. It was a grey, rainy day, but thousands of people gathered on the streets and in St. James's Park to watch the Queen's wedding procession, heralded by a royal salute of 21 guns, from Buckingham Palace to St. James's.

Prince Albert wore a field marshal's uniform, with large rosettes of white satin on his shoulders. The Queen's dress was rich white satin, manufactured in Spitalfields. It was worn off the shoulder and trimmed with orange blossoms; on her head she wore an orange blossom wreath. Her veil was made of Honiton lace and her dress was trimmed with a lace flounce. The lace alone cost over £1,000. Queen Victoria's white wedding dress set a fashion – up to that point white was not a conventional colour for weddings.

As the Queen processed through the various ante-rooms, throne rooms and drawing rooms of St. James's Palace she was observed by 2,100 spectators, who had been issued with tickets for this privileged viewpoint. Queen Victoria was preceded by heralds and trumpeters, officers of the Household, members of the royal family, the Chamberlains and Lord Melbourne bearing the sword of state. Her train, six yards in length, was carried by twelve bridesmaids, dressed in tulle, trimmed with white roses. They were followed by the ladies of the bedchamber, the maids of honour, six gentlemen at arms and the yeomen of the guard. The chapel itself was packed with the great and the good.

The Queen carried a small posy, made up of snowdrops, which were Prince Albert's favourite flower. A myrtle bush was subsequently grown from a cutting brought by Albert from Coburg, and it became a royal tradition to include a sprig of myrtle in the wedding bouquet.

Following the wedding ceremony the couple returned to Buckingham Palace for the wedding breakfast. The main focal point was a wedding cake that weighed nearly 300 lbs and was three yards in circumference.

Queen Victoria's wedding dress was trimmed with Honiton lace and she wore a matching veil. The design of the lace is attributed to William Dyce and a colleague at the Government School of Design in London.

Called Honiton lace, it was really worked at the Devonshire village of Beer, some ten miles from Honiton. It was made under the direction of Miss Bidney, a native of the village, who superintended over 200 lace-workers who took over six months to complete the work. After its completion the pattern was destroyed so that it could never be copied.

The veil was amongst Queen Victoria's most prized possessions and she would eventually be buried with it.

"*Everywhere there was a gorgeous glow of crimson and purple and gold... pennons and streamers attached to tall Venetian masts made the roadsides gay with unwonted colour; tapestry and bunting lined the balconies and strove to hide the dingy fronts of smoke-stained London houses.*"
The Times

The Wedding of Princess May of Teck

PRINCE GEORGE, DUKE OF YORK and Princess May of Teck were married at 12.30pm on 6 July 1893 at the Chapel Royal in St. James's Palace. Princess May had previously been engaged to George's older brother Albert Victor (Eddy), but he died a few weeks after their betrothal. Within a few months George proposed and was accepted.

Princess May (who later was to become Queen Mary) wore a dress of silver and white brocade, embroidered with silver roses, shamrock and thistles. She wore the lace veil in which her mother, Princess Mary, Duchess of Teck, was married, secured with diamond pins and an orange blossom wreath. She carried a bouquet of Provence roses, orchids and orange blossom. Her trousseau consisted partly of "forty outdoor suits, fifteen ball-dresses, five tea-gowns, a vast number of bonnets, shoes, and gloves," according to the *Lady's Pictorial*.

The royal family arrived in a procession of open-topped landaus. Princess May, arriving with her father the Duke of Teck, greeted the crowd with "a nervous gesture of her white-gloved hand". She was attended by ten bridesmaids, all of them princesses: Princess Victoria and Princess Maud of

Wales, sisters of the groom; Princess Victoria and Princess Alexandra of Edinburgh; Princess Victoria of Schleswig-Holstein; Princess Beatrice of Edinburgh, Princess Margaret and Princess Patricia of Connaught; Princess Victoria Eugenie and Princess Alice of Battenberg.

The Archbishop of Canterbury performed the ceremony, assisted by the Bishop of London, the Bishop of Rochester, and five other prelates. About 150 guests were crowded into the royal chapel; amongst them were members of all the main European royal families, including the King and Queen of Denmark, George's maternal grandparents. George and May then made their way to Buckingham Palace, and the marriage register was signed by the Queen, the prime minister, and all other royal personages present.

The wedding was a truly popular pageant, and was attended by huge crowds. Some 4,000 policemen lined the streets as the crowds assembled outside Buckingham Palace in the early hours of the 6th. When the newly married couple appeared on the balcony at Buckingham Palace, the cheering of the crowd was so enthusiastic and prolonged that a chair had to be brought for the elderly Queen Victoria.

Prince George's bride was universally known as Princess May, and only used her given name, Mary, after she became Queen.

The marriage of Prince George, Victoria's grandson, was very much of his grandmother's making. The Queen encouraged him to take an interest in the fiancée of his elder brother, Prince Albert, when she was left alone after his premature death from pneumonia. Prince George proposed to Princess May after a suitable period of mourning, and the marriage was the subject of intense popular enthusiasm.

The couple were both reserved and shy, but they soon became deeply attached to each other. Princess May gave the sometimes gruff and difficult King George V a great deal of support in his new position.

The bridegroom wore the uniform of a captain in the navy.

The bride's lace veil floated backwards, leaving her face in full view. Her diamond tiara was a wedding gift from Queen Victoria. She wore a diamond rivière necklace, set off by diamond earrings and a diamond anchor brooch.

"The warm and generous heart of this people takes you today unto itself. Will you not, in response, take that heart, with all its joys and sorrows, unto your own?"
Cosmo Lang, Archbishop of Canterbury

The Wedding of Lady Elizabeth Bowes-Lyon

THE WEDDING OF HRH the Duke of York and Lady Elizabeth Bowes-Lyon was celebrated on 26 April 1923 at Westminster Abbey. The wedding procession was led by the Archbishop of Canterbury, the Archbishop of York, Bishop of London and Primate of Scotland; they were followed by key members of the royal family.

The Duke of York, known as Bertie, arrived at the Abbey accompanied by his brothers the Prince of Wales and Prince Henry. He wore his Royal Air Force Group Captain's uniform. The arrival of the bride was heralded by cheers. As Lady Elizabeth and her father passed the Tomb of the Unknown Soldier, the bride spontaneously laid her bouquet of white roses on the tomb, perhaps remembering her own brother, Fergus, who was a casualty of the Great War. This was the start of a royal tradition that persisted throughout the 20th century.

Elizabeth's procession down the aisle was to the boys' choir, singing 'Lead us, Heavenly Father'. The choir sang 'Beloved, Let us Love One Another', which had been composed by the Westminster Abbey organist Sir Sydney Hugo Nicholson for the wedding of Princess Mary the previous year. The newly-married couple proceeded up the Abbey aisle to Mendelssohn's Wedding March.

Lady Elizabeth was the recipient of some spectacular jewellery. Bertie had given her a large oval sapphire engagement ring from Kashmir, surrounded by diamonds. Her father, the Earl of Strathmore, gave her a platinum and diamond tiara. George V presented her with a diamond ribbon bow brooch. Her wedding dress, designed by Madame Handley-Seymour of New Bond Street, was a classically simple design that reflected the boyish fashions of the day. It was a gown of ivory tinted chiffon moiré, embroidered with pearls. The veil, of 'point de Flandres' (bobbin-made lace) was loaned to her by Queen Mary. The train was of machine-made lace from Nottingham, a royal gesture of support to the factory workers.

The wedding breakfast, held at Buckingham Palace, comprised: Consommé a la Windsor, Suprêmes de Saumon Reine Mary, Côtelettes d'Agneau Prince Albert, Chapons à la Strathmore, Jambon et Langue Découpés à l'Aspic, Salade Royale, Asperges, Sauce Crème Mousseuse, Fraises Duchesse Elizabeth, Panier de Friandises, Dessert, Café.

Lady Elizabeth had an escort of eight bridesmaids: her nieces the Hon Elizabeth Elphinstone and the Hon Cecilia Bowes-Lyon, Lady May Cambridge and Lady Mary Cambridge, both cousins of the groom, Lady Katherine Hamilton, Lady Mary Thynne, the Hon Diamond Hardinge and Miss Elizabeth Cator, who would go on to marry Elizabeth's brother Michael.

Her bridesmaids, the leading debutantes of the day, were celebrated in this double-page spread from the weekly magazine, *The Bystander* (left).

Lady Elizabeth had nursed wounded soldiers during the Great War, and came out as a debutante after the armistice. She met the Duke of York at a round of society balls and functions in the early 1920s.

"I was so proud of you & thrilled at having you so close to me on our long walk in Westminster Abbey, but when I handed your hand to the Archbishop I felt I had lost something very precious. You were so calm and composed during the Service & said your words with such conviction, that I knew everything was all right." George VI in a letter to Princess Elizabeth

The Wedding of Princess Elizabeth

PRINCESS ELIZABETH'S WEDDING was a perfect antidote to the austerity of post-war Britain. The wedding pageant was a theatrical celebration of youth, glamour and hope, symbolising renaissance and recovery.

More than 2,000 guests were in attendance as Elizabeth and Philip became husband and wife at Westminster Abbey on 20 November 1947. The first royal festivity since the end of the Second World War, the wedding was celebrated across the country. Eight bridesmaids and two pageboys took part in the ceremony, which was officiated by both the Archbishop of Canterbury and the Archbishop of York.

Less than three months before the wedding date, Norman Hartnell was named as the dress designer. He found inspiration in a Botticelli figure and set to work. The dress was made of satin woven at the Scottish firm of Winterthur near Dunfermline. Difficulties arose when rivals put about the rumour that the Scottish satin was made from 'enemy silk worms', either from Italy or possibly Japan. A telephone call to Dunfermline soon confirmed that the silk had in fact come from Chinese silkworms at Lullingstone Castle, and patriotic post-war anxieties were assuaged.

It is widely reported that Princess Elizabeth had to save up her clothing rations to purchase the material for the dress. The Government had given her 200 extra clothing coupons as a contribution towards her trousseau – a gift to all British brides at that time. The richly embroidered white satin dress included representations of flora from the British Isles and Commonwealth: Irish shamrocks, Scottish thistles, Canadian maple leaves and English Tudor roses.

It was Princess Elizabeth's wish that the solemnisation of the marriage should be taken from the Book of Common Prayer, including the vow to 'obey' her husband. In a rousing address the Archbishop of York told the couple "With high and confident hope for all that this day means for yourselves and the nation, we send you forth from the Abbey to the great multitudes outside."

After the wedding ceremony, a wedding breakfast for 150 guests was held at Buckingham Palace where each was presented with a posy of white heather and myrtle as favours. On the menu was a casserole of unrationed partridges, with Filet de Sole Mountbatten to start and Bombe Glacée Princess Elizabeth as dessert.

Shimmering garlands of orange blossom, syringa, jasmine and white Rose of York were worked into the 15-foot train in pearl and diamante. The bride's lace train and veil boasted more than 100 miles of gossamer silk thread. The bride wore a diamond tiara made for Queen Mary in 1919.

The two royal kneelers, used during the service, were covered in rose pink silk. They were made from orange boxes, due to wartime austerity, and date stamped 1946.

The hymns were 'Praise my Soul, the King of Heaven' and 'The Lord's my Shepherd' and the couple left the Church to Mendelssohn's Wedding March.

"In my own sort of humble way I have always tried to take some part of the burden off my sister. She can't do it all, you know. I leap at the opportunity of doing lots of different things to help." Princess Margaret

The Wedding of Princess Margaret

THE MARRIAGE OF Princess Margaret and Antony Armstrong-Jones (made Earl Snowdon on his wedding day) was celebrated at Westminster Abbey on 6 May 1960. It was the first-ever televised royal wedding service, attracting more than 300 million viewers worldwide.

Princess Margaret was given away by the Duke of Edinburgh, and made the journey by traditional glass coach from Clarence House to the Abbey on a sunny spring day. Inside the church were 2,000 guests, and an innovative CCTV system that enabled guests in all parts of the Abbey to see the service in the sanctuary. A loudspeaker system broadcast the proceedings to the huge crowd outside.

Princess Margaret wore a dress of white silk organza, with a high neckline, cinched waist, tight-fitting bodice, and billowing ballgown skirts. It was designed by Norman Hartnell, who was also responsible for the Queen's wedding dress. The dress flattered her petite figure, and did not rely on embellishments to accentuate her beauty. Unlike previous royal wedding dresses, there was no court train; instead the skirt itself formed a short court train. She wore the famous Poltimore diamond tiara, to which

a veil of silk organza, made by Claude St. Cyr of Paris, was attached, and carried a bouquet of orchids, freesia, stephanotis, and lily of the valley.

Her eight bridesmaids, all aged under 12, were led by Princess Anne. The bridesmaids' dresses, also by Hartnell, were replicas of Princess Margaret's first evening dress, a great favourite of her father's. They were flounced, with insets of broderie anglaise, and trimmed with blue ribbon. A young Prince Charles, also a member of the wedding party, was dressed in a tartan kilt and ruffled cravat.

Trumpets heralded the Princess's arrival at the Abbey, and she walked up the aisle to the strains of 'Christ is Made the Sure Foundation'. The traditional service was led by the Archbishop of Canterbury, Dr Geoffrey Fisher.

The wedding breakfast was attended by 120 guests. Her cake, which was made by J. Lyons, took five weeks to complete, was 5 feet tall and weighed 150 lbs. The cake was decorated with white sugar panels piped in oak leaf design. Princess Margaret's coat of arms and the initials of the bride and groom were incorporated in the design.

The princess's wedding dress was the height of early sixties fashion, and the wedding (*top*) epitomised the voguish glamour of the couple.

Princess Margaret looked radiant in her Poltimore tiara, which had been purchased for her at auction for over £5,000. It had originally been made by Garrard in 1870, and could be transformed into a necklace and eleven scroll brooches. On her wedding day her hairdresser styled her hair into a chic chignon, to give her height, and her veil was held in place by the tiara. The tiara was sold in 2006 at a Christie's auction for over a million pounds.

The princess also wore a diamond rivière necklace, which she had inherited from her grandmother, Queen Mary, in 1953.

"Here is the stuff of which fairy tales are made: the Prince and Princess on their wedding day. Those who are married live happily ever after the wedding day if they persevere in the real adventure which is the royal task of creating each other and creating a more loving world."

Robert Runcie, Archbishop of Canterbury

The Wedding of Lady Diana Spencer

PRINCE CHARLES and Lady Diana Spencer were married on 29 July 1981. This eagerly awaited event was a national holiday and crowds of 600,000 filled the London streets, eager to catch a glimpse of the royal couple. An estimated 750 million viewers watched the wedding worldwide.

In a break from royal tradition, St. Paul's Cathedral was chosen by the groom as the venue. The bride journeyed from Clarence House to St. Paul's in a glass coach, wearing a silk taffeta, hand-embroidered puffball dress, with exaggerated puffed sleeves and a frilly neckline, designed by Elizabeth and David Emanuel. The 25-foot long train, somewhat creased by the cramped interior of the coach, took some time to arrange on the steps of the cathedral. She was attended by four bridesmaids and two pages. Lady Sarah Armstrong-Jones was her maid of honour.

In front of a congregation of 3,500 people, and accompanied by a dramatic Trumpet Voluntary, Diana walked down the aisle on the arm of her father, Earl Spencer – a journey of three-and-a-half minutes – to the altar where Prince Charles was waiting. He wore the Navy's No. 1 ceremonial dress uniform, with a blue garter

sash. The Dean of St. Paul's introduced the service, which was conducted by the Archbishop of Canterbury. Diana did not promise to 'obey', as royal brides in the past had done. The bride's nerves showed briefly when she mixed up the Prince's names, calling him Philip Charles, rather than Charles Philip.

After signing the register, the royal couple returned to the altar while Dame Kiri Te Kanawa sang Handel's 'Let the Bright Seraphim'. The couple left the cathedral to the strain of Elgar's 'Pomp and Circumstance March No 4 in G' and 'Crown Imperial'. Their journey in a 1902 landau through the streets of the City of London to Buckingham Palace was accompanied by the jubilant chimes of bells from churches all over London.

On the balcony at Buckingham Palace, the couple delighted the crowd with a kiss – a departure from the formality of previous royal balcony appearances. A traditional wedding breakfast followed, where guests dined on brill in lobster sauce, chicken breasts and strawberries and Cornish cream. The five-tiered, 225-pound hexagonal wedding cake was cut by Prince Charles, using his ceremonial sword.

The newly-weds emerge from St. Paul's Cathedral. Diana's billowing gown and spectacular 25-foot train was to become a much-copied 1980s classic.

Her cascading bouquet, an intricate confection of gardenias, lilies of the valley, white freesia, golden roses, white orchids and stephanotis. was 42 inches long, and was a gift from the Worshipful Company of Gardeners.

Diana's ivory silk-taffeta and vintage-lace dress had a fitted, boned bodice. Its most outstanding features were the puffed sleeves, decorated with hundreds of tiny ribbons. The dress shimmered with 10,000 hand-sewn pieces of pearl and mother-of-pearl sequins. Taffeta bows decorated the neckline.

Diana wore the Spencer family tiara and her mother's diamond earrings (something borrowed). The 'something old' was a piece of Carrickmacross lace on the bodice which had belonged to Queen Mary, and for 'something blue', the Emanuels, the dress designers, had hand-sewn a little blue bow into the back of the dress, as well as adding a gold horseshoe for luck.

"Like all the best families, we have our share of eccentricities, of impetuous and wayward youngsters and of family disagreements."
Queen Elizabeth II

Other Members of the Royal Family

THE WEDDINGS OF the Queen's daughter and two younger sons have been a series of landmark events that have spanned three decades. Princess Anne was the first of the Queen's children to marry, at Westminster Abbey, on 14 November 1973. She wore a high-collared Tudor style gown with full medieval sleeves, and her husband Lieutenant Mark Phillips wore the full scarlet and blue uniform of the Queen's Dragoon Guards. There was an estimated worldwide television audience of 500 million, and the wedding day was declared a public holiday.

On 23 July 1986 Prince Andrew married Sarah Ferguson at Westminster Abbey. The Queen conferred Prince Andrew with the title Duke of York – last held by King George VI and traditionally reserved for the sovereign's second son – just 90 minutes before the ceremony.

The ceremony took place in front of 2,000 people, including 17 representatives of foreign royalty and the US president Ronald Reagan and his wife Nancy. Sarah Ferguson's spectacular wedding dress was designed by Lindka Cierach and was made from heavy ivory duchesse satin, which was manufactured at Britain's only silk farm,

Lullingstone near Sherborne in Dorset. With a Renaissance silhouette and full sleeves, the dress was set off by a magnificent train, elaborately embroidered with designs of thistles and bees, symbols on Sarah's coat of arms, as well as anchors and waves, alluding to Andrew's naval career. The bride, unlike Diana, opted to 'love, honour and obey'.

The newly weds were transported back to the Palace in a turn-of-the-century landau, and delighted crowds with a playful balcony kiss. At the wedding breakfast, a traditional meal of lobster and lamb was served, and there was a 6-ft tall white wedding cake, decorated wth pastel flowers.

Prince Edward married his long-time partner Sophie Rhys-Jones on 19 June 1999 at St. George's Chapel, Windsor Castle. The Queen had conferred the title of Earl of Wessex on her youngest son. The service was low key by royal standards, but Sophie's silk organza and silk crepe coat dress was simple and elegant. She wore a silk tulle veil, decorated with crystals, fastened to a diamond tiara that was loaned by Queen Elizabeth. The groom wore a morning coat by John Kent, adding a splash of colour with a yellow waistcoat and blue tie.

Sarah Ferguson enjoys a private moment with her father Major Ronald Ferguson. She wore a headdress of fresh flowers – roses, lily petals, gardenias (Andrew's favourite flower) and lilies of the valley. At the end of the ceremony the headdress was removed to reveal a diamond tiara, symbolic of her metamorphosis from commoner to royal. In Sarah's words, "I had stepped up as the country girl; I would walk back as a princess."

Prince Edward and Sophie Rhys-Jones delighted crowds on the streets of Windsor as they drove in an open Ascot landau carriage through the precincts of Windsor Castle before travelling along Windsor High Street and Park Street.

The intimate 14th-century chapel at Windsor was an unusual choice of venues – most major royal weddings have taken place in the capital.

Wedding Traditions

The magnificence of royal weddings, which have captivated the general public with their pomp and ceremony, is underlain with a series of traditions that have evolved over the last two centuries. From the fairytale glass coach that conveys the bride to the church to the sprig of myrtle in the bridal bouquet (subsequently laid on the tomb of the unknown soldier) and the wedding ring made of Welsh gold, these traditions have been cherished by successive royal couples.

The day before her wedding, Queen Victoria recorded the gift from "dearest Albert" of "a splendid brooch, a large sapphire set round with diamonds, which is really quite beautiful".

Wedding Jewellery

SAPPHIRES, SYMBOLIC OF TRUST AND LOYALTY, have played an important role in royal weddings. Queen Victoria was captivated by Albert's wedding gift of a sapphire and diamond brooch, and wore it on the front of her dress (*see page 27*).

The tradition of giving sapphire engagement rings is also well established. The Queen Mother was given a magnificent Kashmiri sapphire engagement ring, and many other royal brides, including Princess Anne and Princess Michael of Kent have also worn sapphire rings. Perhaps the most famous of all is Princess Diana's sapphire engagement ring, encircled by 14 diamonds, which Prince William has now passed on to Catherine Middleton. The Queen's engagement ring uses diamonds from a tiara that once belonged to Prince Philip's mother. Both Princess Margaret and Sarah Ferguson shared the less conventional option of ruby engagement rings.

Another royal tradition, originating with the Queen Mother, is for the wedding ring to be made from gold from the Clogau St. David's mine in Wales (*right*). The Queen was presented with a 1kg gold nugget from the company's Bontddu mine in 1986. The gold, stained by the copper ore which is also found in the mine, has a unique pink tinge.

This magnificent brooch, consisting of a single sapphire surrounded by diamonds, was probably commissioned from a London jeweller, such as Kitching & Abud or Mortimer & Hunt, by Prince Albert. Queen Victoria wore it, along with a necklace and earrings of Turkish diamonds, presented by the Sultan in 1838, on her wedding day.

Detail: Queen Victoria's sapphire and diamond wedding brooch

"I roamed the London Art Galleries in search of classic inspiration and fortunately found a Botticelli figure in clinging ivory silk, trailed with jasmine, smilax, syringa and small white rose-like blossoms. I thought these flora might be interpreted on a modern dress through the medium of white crystals and pearls." Norman Hartnell

Wedding Dresses

ROYAL WEDDING DRESSES do not merely showcase the beauty of the bride, they also display local crafts skills to the world. Queen Victoria revived the declining Honiton Lace industry, based in East Devon, by ordering a great deal of ceremonial lace, including that used for her wedding veil.

Elizabeth II's Hartnell-designed gown and star-patterened train was inspired Botticelli's *Primavera*, symbolic of Britain's renaissance after the austerity of the Second World War. The gown was heavily embroidered with 10,000 seed pearls (flown in from the United States), silver thread, crystals, and tulle appliqués. The duchesse satin was resistant to creasing and was both architectural and fluid, providing enough weight for the embroidery. It was woven at Winterthur Silks Limited, Dunfermline, in the Canmore factory, using silk that had come from Chinese silkworms at Lullingstone Castle.

The Queen Mother's gown (*right*) was made of ivory chiffon moiré. The bodice was enhanced with pearls and elaborate silver embroidery. It featured a dropped waist and a full length embroidered skirt. Nottingham lace-workers (*top*) were enlisted to complete her trousseau, including 65 formal gowns, over a hundred dresses and 72 fur coats and hats.

Princess Elizabeth's wedding dress was made of ivory duchess satin in the 'Princess' style with a fitted bodice. The neckline had a deep-scalloped edge. The front bodice was cut in three panels and the back cut in four, fastening down the centre back with buttons and loops. The wrist-length, tight-fitting sleeves ended in embroidered cuffs. From the low-pointed waist, the skirt, cut on the cross, extended to a deep circular train.

Detail: Front view of Princess Elizabeth's wedding dress

Dress Design

THE DESIGN OF ROYAL wedding dresses is a closely guarded secret, subject of much speculation in the months leading up to the big day, and even some subterfuge.

Norman Hartnell, who designed Elizabeth II's wedding dress in 1947, her coronation gown in 1953 and Princess Margaret's wedding dress in 1960, became one of the most famous couturiers in the world, thanks to royal patronage. Known for his elaborately embroidered evening gowns, his breakthrough came in 1938, when he designed an entire wardrobe for the Queen Mother's state visit to France.

When Norman Hartnell was commissioned to create Princess Elizabeth's wedding dress he whitewashed his workshop windows to prevent spying. 350 girls worked on the gown for seven weeks in absolute secrecy. He managed to keep the design of the dress from the press, whose only glimpse of it was the 4-ft-high box in which it was packed for its journey from his salon on the day before the wedding.

The media frenzy that surrounded Princess Diana's wedding dress was even more pronounced. The dress designers, Elizabeth and David Emanuel, had only been out of college

a year when they received the momentous call. The couple had only three months to complete the commission, and they were still working on it on the evening before the wedding. Speculation over every detail of the wedding dress was so intense the Emanuels hired two full-time security guards and began to play a game of double bluff with nosy reporters. They put decoy scraps of fabric and thread in the rubbish bins and hung up a spare dress to fool the curious. Their famous client had a code name (Deborah) and amazed the designers by tending to most design details on her own.

Lesotho-born Lindka Cierach's first commission was for a Bahrain princess, but she really hit the headlines when she designed Sarah Ferguson's wedding dress in 1986 (*top left*). She had to paste metallic covering film to her studio windows in South Kensington to obstruct photographers. She said: "Of course, friends and staff were offered money for information, but everybody was very honourable and I got amazing support from the police."

When Samantha Shaw was commissioned to design Sophie Rhys Jones's wedding dress in 1999 she avoided all these dramas by quietly withdrawing to a secret location.

An array of designs for the wedding dresses of the century. Clockwise from top: Norman Hartnell's sketch for Princess Margaret's silk organza dress, the Emanuels' designs for Diana's 'meringue dress', front and back views of Cierach's dress for Sarah Ferguson, another view of Diana's dress and (below) Hartnell's design for the Queen's wedding dress.

Details: Designs and sketches for four iconic royal wedding dresses

47

"The Queen is the only person who can put on a tiara with one hand, while walking down stairs." Princess Margaret

Wedding Tiaras

TIARAS ARE INTEGRAL to royal weddings. They are not only a magnificent adornment for the bride, but they are also frequently given as wedding presents, or loaned to new brides from the Queen's extensive collection. Tiaras are used to secure the wedding veil, which is a traditional feature of all royal weddings. It is the custom for brides marrying into the royal family to cover the face; those already in the royal family leave the face exposed.

The Cambridge Lovers' knot tiara (*above*) has had a particularly interesting journey. It was originally owned by Queen Mary, and was created to her own specifications in 1913 by the jewellers Garrards, using diamonds and pearls from Queen Mary's collection. The tiara consisted of 19 arches, and 38 drop-shaped pearls, 19 hanging as pendants and 19 rising up as spikes. Queen Mary was able to remove and add the pearls that rose up as spikes, as and when she deemed fit.

When Queen Mary died in 1953 she left the Cambridge Lovers' knot tiara to her grand-daughter, Queen Elizabeth II. The Queen wore the tiara on many state occasions, and presented it to Princess Diana as a wedding gift. The tiara

became closely associated with the glamourous image of the popular princess. After Diana's divorce from Prince Charles, the tiara was returned to Her Majesty the Queen.

Queen Mary was a notable collector of *objets d'art* and jewellery, and added many pieces to the Royal Collection. Her wedding in 1893 was an occasion for the most flamboyant of wedding presents, which flooded in from all the crowned heads of Europe. She received a vast array of exquisite bracelets, brooches, rings, pendants and necklaces from her own family and members of the aristocracy. Among these was the famous Girls of Great Britain and Ireland tiara, purchased from London jeweller Garrards by a committee organised by Lady Eva Greville. It was given to Princess Elizabeth on her wedding day, and is now very familiar from images of Her Majesty on banknotes and coinage.

When Princess Elizabeth was married she wore the 'Queen Mary's fringe tiara', which had been commissioned by Queen Mary in 1919 and made from a diamond necklace she received from Queen Victoria as a wedding present, which was purchased from Collingwood & Co. jewellers in 1893. The tiara was lent to Princess Anne for her wedding in 1973.

Princess Diana was married in the Spencer family tiara, an elaborate design of stylised diamond-studded flowers in a silver setting. The tiara was created from different pieces belonging to the Spencer family in the 19th century, and was remodelled in 1935. Her brother, Earl Spencer, intimated that, on the day of the wedding, wearing the unfamiliar tiara had given the princess a 'cracking headache'.

Detail: Diana wears 'something borrowed', the Spencer family tiara

"Elegance and comfort are not incompatible, and whoever maintains the contrary simply doesn't know what he's talking about."
Salvatore Ferragamo

Wedding Shoes

SEMI-CONCEALED BENEATH the wedding dress, shoes still play an important part of the bridal ensemble, and great trouble is taken with them.

Although Queen Victoria was very small, and her feet were only 9 inches long (her shoe size was a mere 3½) she wore, in the fashion of the times, completely flat slippers. In the 19th century ladies' feet were considered unattractive, and shoes were designed so they were completely concealed by the sweeping hemline of the dress.

Princess Elizabeth and Princess Margaret, both petite, wore heels to give them additional height. Princess Diana, on the other hand, was 5ft 10in tall, so flat shoes were more appropriate. She wore a pair of wedding slippers designed by Clive Shilton of embroidered ivory silk decorated with mother of pearl sequins. There were heart-shaped lace rosettes on the uppers of each shoe. On the hand-made tooled leather sole there was a gold and a fleurette pattern including the CD insignia with a heart. Two pairs of slippers were made for her in case of emergencies. Sarah Ferguson's wedding shoes, designed by Manolo Blahnik, featured a beaded bee design that complemented her dress.

Elizabeth Bowes-Lyon's ivory satin wedding shoes were embellished with embroidery, and their T-bar design was typical of the 'flapper' fashions of the 1920s.

Princess Elizabeth's wedding shoes were ivory duchesse satin embellished with silver and pearls. They had reasonably low heels and a small platform, giving her height, but ensuring she was comfortable as well.

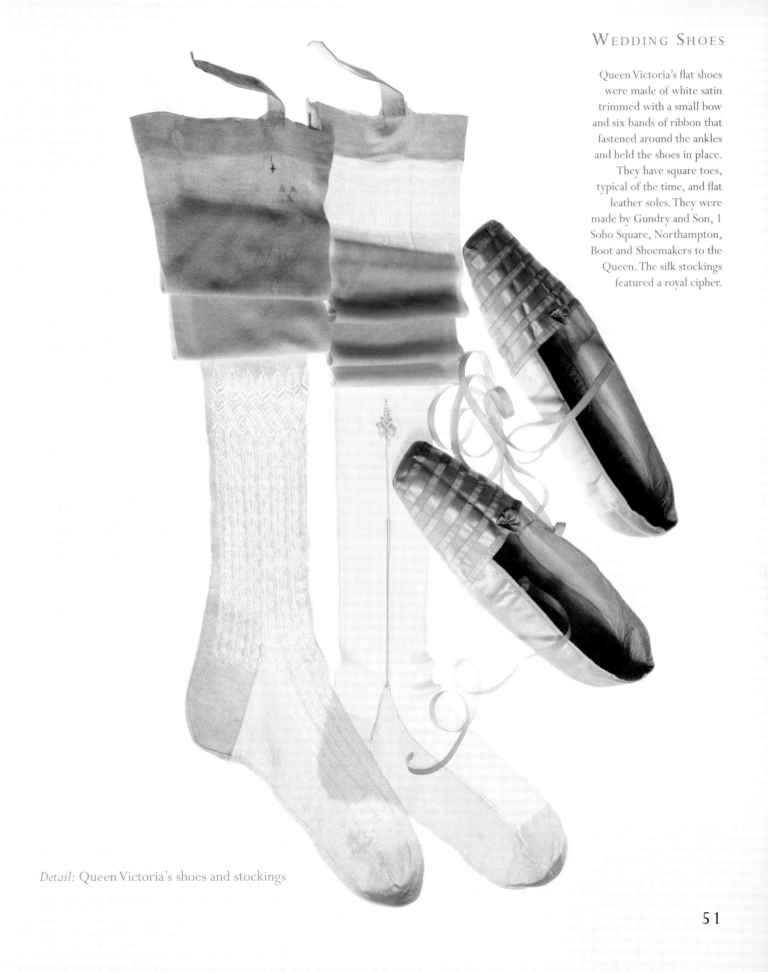

Queen Victoria's flat shoes were made of white satin trimmed with a small bow and six bands of ribbon that fastened around the ankles and held the shoes in place. They have square toes, typical of the time, and flat leather soles. They were made by Gundry and Son, 1 Soho Square, Northampton, Boot and Shoemakers to the Queen. The silk stockings featured a royal cipher.

Detail: Queen Victoria's shoes and stockings

At her wedding to Prince
Charles, Camilla Parker
Bowles carried a bouquet of
lily of the valley and yellow,
purple and white primroses
with a sprig of myrtle,
sent by a well-wisher from
Cornwall.

Wedding Bouquets

ROYAL BRIDES have carried an array of beautiful bouquets
on their wedding day, frequently featuring myrtle, roses,
orchids, stephanotis, gardenias and lilies of the valley. Royal
bridal bouquets are predominantly white: Queen Victoria,
who was married in February, had snowdrops, Elizabeth
Bowes-Lyon carried a bouquet of lily of the valley and the
Queen carried a bouquet of home-grown orchids.

Many royal wedding bouquets have been made from flowers
presented by the Worshipful Company of Gardeners, a royal
livery company with origins dating to the 14th century, and
a Royal Charter dated 1605. Longmans florists have been
responsible for making the wedding bouquets of a succession of
royal brides, including Princess Elizabeth, Princess Margaret,
the Duchess of Kent, Princess Michael, Princess Alexandra and
Princess Diana.

Princess Elizabeth's orchid bouquet went missing after her
return from the Abbey, probably placed by an over-zealous
footman in a cold cupboard, and photographs taken on the day
show her empty-handed. A replica bouquet was commissioned
and photographs were re-taken. It is now common practice to
have two or three bouquets made.

Princess Anne's wedding bouquet consisted of white roses, lilies of the valley, and stephanotis, with a sprig of white heather for luck. Princess Diana's shower style bouquet contained roses, gardenia, stephanotis and orchids. Sophie Rhys-Jones's cascading bouquet was an arrangement of blown ivory garden roses, scented stephanotis, clustered lily of the valley and ivory freesia.

Details: Three royal bridal bouquets, each including a traditional sprig of myrtle

Queen Victoria's wedding cake was reportedly nine feet in circumference, weighed 300 pounds and was adorned with roses. An ice sculpture of Britannia surrounded by cupids capped the cake. Thousands of wedding cake boxes were given to guests or sent as souvenirs: Victoria was related to all the royal families of Europe, and all would have expected a piece. Several extra cakes were made to cope with the demand.

Wedding Cakes

ROYAL WEDDING CAKES are not only a magnificent adornment to the day itself – slices of the cake are also sent as gifts all over the world. This tradition, which started with Queen Victoria, continues to the present day.

The present Queen's official wedding cake (*right*) was made by McVitie & Price of Edinburgh. Eleven other cakes were given as presents. With post-war food rationing still in place ingredients were sent as wedding presents from overseas, for example the official cake was made using ingredients given by Australian Girl Guides. Pieces of cake and food parcels were later distributed to schoolchildren and institutions.

The four-tiered cake was nine feet high and weighed 500 pounds. It was decorated with painted panels of the armorial bearings of both families, and included the monograms of bride and groom, sugar-iced figures to depict their favourite activities, and regimental and naval badges. Round the sides of the cakes were delicate, curved 'galleries', reminiscent of the turrets on Scottish castles, beloved by the royal family. The cake was cut using the Duke of Edinburgh's Mountbatten sword, a wedding present from the King. In 1981 Prince Charles also used a ceremonial sword to cut the wedding cake.

People queued around the block outside Huntley and Palmers in Reading, Berkshire, to see the royal wedding cake baked for the marriage of the Duke of York and Elizabeth Bowes-Lyon in 1923. The cake was 10 feet high, weighed 800 pounds, was filled with real gold charms and was topped by these delicate winged putti holding wedding rings.

Detail: Figurines from the Wedding Cake of Elizabeth Bowes-Lyon

"*I remember the moment she appeared at the top of the stairs. Everyone fell silent. She was radiant and ready to become the most famous of princesses.*" India Hicks, one of Princess Diana's four bridesmaids

Royal Bridesmaids

Until the middle of the 20th century bridesmaids at royal weddings were grown women, usually coming from the upper ranks of the aristocracy or fellow royals. Queen Victoria had twelve bridesmaids carrying her train, all the eldest daughters of peers. The Queen herself designed the bridesmaids' dresses, sketching a simple white dress trimmed with sprays of roses attached to the bodice, the skirt and in the hair. Each of the bridesmaids was presented with a brooch by the royal couple: these were eagle-shaped, and made of turquoises and pearls (representing true love), rubies for passion and diamonds for eternity.

Each of Princess May of Teck's bridesmaids was a princess, while Elizabeth Bowes-Lyons's choices were an array of the leading debutantes of the day. Her nieces Elizabeth Elphinstone, and Cecilia Bowes-Lyon carried her train. Her bridesmaids' dresses were made of white chiffon Nottingham lace. In their hair, they wore green myrtle leaves and a white rose with a sprig of white heather.

Princess Elizabeth had eight bridesmaids, led by her younger sister, Prince Margaret. The youngest bridesmaid was Princess Alexandra, aged twelve. Their dresses, designed by Norman

Hartnell, incorporated the Primavera-inspired decorations that adorned the bridal dress. They wore wreaths in their hair of miniature white sheaves, lilies and London Pride, modelled in white satin and silver lame. To mark the day, Prince Philip gave the bridesmaids a silver and rose-gold powder compact that he had designed himself.

Princess Margaret moved away from the tradition of adult bridesmaids, with eight bridesmaids, ranging in age from six to twelve; Princess Anne, aged nine, was amongst them. They wore ballerina dresses, designed by Norman Hartnell (*top left*), trimmed with broderie anglaise and blue ribbon.

Princess Diana chose an exceptionally young bridesmaid, Clementine Hambro, who was only five (the dress designer Elizabeth Emanuel recalled "we all fell in love with Clem"). Her three fellow bridesmaids were aged from six to 14. Princess Margaret's daughter, 17-year-old Lady Sarah Armstrong-Jones, was the maid of honour. She, along with India Hicks, had the unenviable task of handling Diana's daunting 25-ft train. The girls were dressed in the same fabric as Diana's wedding dress, but in a lighter weight. The dresses were trimmed in taffeta and lace.

Princess Diana exchanges words with her youngest bridesmaid, five-year-old Clementine Hambro, while the Queen looks on. In the foreground stands Lady Sarah Armstrong-Jones (now Lady Sarah Chatto), the maid of honour, who wore a full length dress. The younger girls wore ballerina-length dresses and flat pumps with a delicate strap. They carried wooden hoops festooned with flowers, with circlets of flowers in their hair. Lady Sarah carried a loose posy of garden flowers.

After the wedding breakfast and cake-cutting, the bridesmaids helped Diana change into her going-away outfit, and she gave each of them a gift – a delicate china pot containing two silkworms that had spun the silk for her wedding dress.

A pageboy is a young male attendant, frequently seen at royal weddings. They are often younger brothers or nephews of the bride or groom. Traditionally, they carry the bride's train, although very young boys are never given responsibility for the magnificent trains worn at royal weddings.

Royal Pages

ALTHOUGH HISTORICALLY small boys have played a less important role in royal weddings, there has been a growing tradition to include young boys in the bridal party.

This change started with Princess Elizabeth, who had two pageboys at her 1947 wedding to Prince Philip: Prince William of Gloucester and Prince Michael of Kent. Aged just six and five respectively, the two small boys in their kilts and sporrans were a delightful contrast to the glamorous grown-up bridesmaids.

When Princess Anne got married in 1973 her pure silk gauze train was carried by her pageboy Prince Edward and bridesmaid, Lady Sarah Armstrong-Jones. Prince Edward, her youngest brother, was nine at the time. Like her mother before her, Anne chose a kilt, sporran and frilled shirt ensemble for her pageboy.

At the wedding of Lady Diana and Prince Charles the two young pageboys played a symbolic role, their outfits referring back to the year 1863, the last occasion on which a Prince of Wales had been married. The pageboys were Edward van Cutsem, aged eight, the son of Charles's

racehorse training friends Hugh and Emilie van Cutsem; and eleven-year-old Lord Nicholas Windsor, Charles's godson and the son of the Duke and Duchess of Kent.

The pageboys wore full dress Royal Navy summer uniforms from 1863. These consisted of a full dress tailcoat in indigo blue cloth, with naval buttons on the chest, cuffs and pockets and white trousers. They carried a gold-hilted dirk (or dagger), which hung from their belts. Their caps were embellished with a gold wire emboidered badge.

When Prince Edward married Sophie Rhys-Jones in 1999 they chose two bridesmaids, and two pages, all of whom were their godchildren. The two pageboys (*top left*) Felix Sowerbutts (aged seven) and Harry Warburton (aged six) wore ivory silk taffeta long-sleeved shirts with covered buttons at the front, navy velvet knickerbockers with brass-button details and taffeta cummerbunds. Their clothes were designed by Sophie's dress designer, Samantha Shaw.

They also wore velvet tunics, which matched the bridesmaids' tunics except with Nehru collars, white tights and black buckled patent shoes.

Princess Elizabeth's two pageboys, Prince Michael of Kent and Prince William of Gloucester, were dressed in frilled white shirts, Royal Stuart tartan kilts, buckled shoes and white socks. They are pictured here wrapped in warm woollen shawls – the wedding took place on a chilly November day.

Prince Michael of Kent (*left*) is a grandson of King George V and Queen Mary, and is a cousin of both the Queen and the Duke of Edinburgh. Prince William of Gloucester (*right*) was another grandson of King George V and a first cousin of the Queen. He was killed in a light aircraft crash in 1972.

When Prince Andrew and Sarah Ferguson married in 1986 they had four pageboys; the youngest, Prince William, was only four. Prince Andrew, resplendent in naval uniform, was complemented by the pageboys, who wore Victorian-style sailor suits, complete with straw boaters.

The service probably seemed interminable to Prince William, who seems more interested in his cousin Laura Fellowes, a niece of Princess Diana's, than the proceedings at the altar.

When Prince Andrew and Sarah Ferguson left for their honeymoon in the Azores in a horse-drawn carriage they discovered that someone, probably Prince Edward, had left a giant bear inside. In the words of Prince Andrew, "I've got a teddy bear collection from all over the world of one sort or another."

Going Away

THE FINAL RITUAL OF THE royal wedding day is the departure for the honeymoon. Historically, royal honeymoons have been quite low-key and domestic affairs, a simple withdrawal from the attention of the press and public.

Queen Victoria and Prince Albert left their wedding breakfast at about 4pm, and boarded a simple stagecoach. With an escort of three small coaches, they made their way to Windsor Castle. Crowds lined the route and the boys of Eton College turned out to cheer them along. After just a day on their own, Queen Victoria organised two dances on two consecutive nights – regarded as a terrible breach of etiquette by the grand ladies of the Court.

Princess May of Teck changed from her bridal gown into a dress of white Irish poplin embroidered with gold cord. The newly-weds travelled in an open carriage to Liverpool Street, and took a train to Norfolk, where they enjoyed a honeymoon at York Cottage on the Sandringham estate, which the Queen had given them as a wedding present.

Elizabeth Bowes-Lyon and the Duke of York joined a house party given by the hostess Mrs Ronald Greville at

Polesden Lacey in Surrey, and then made their way to her ancestral home in Scotland, Glamis Castle, for the rest of their honeymoon. Princess Elizabeth followed a similar pattern when she married in 1947. Dressed in a going away outfit designed by Norman Hartnell, a blue velvet coat and matching beret trimmed with ostrich feathers, the princess and Prince Philip were tucked into an open carriage with hot water bottles and her favourite corgi, Susan, for their journey to Waterloo Station. They were showered with rose petals. They spent a few days at Broadlands, the Mountbattens' house in Hampshire, before going on to Birkhall on the Balmoral estate.

Princess Diana's going away outfit was a customised pink suit by David Sassoon of Belleville Sassoon. Charles and Diana also took a carriage to Waterloo, and from there to Broadlands. The second part of their honeymoon was spent on the Royal Yacht Britannia, which they joined at Gibraltar. They cruised, pursued by an eager press pack, to Algeria, Tunisia, Sicily, the Greek islands and finally, Egypt. The third, and final, part of their honeymoon was spent at Balmoral. The honeymoon ended three months after the wedding, when public engagements resumed.

A family affair: members of the royal party, including the Queen, the Queen Mother (in full-length court dress), the bridesmaids and pages, run after the departing car that took Princess Margaret and Lord Snowdon to the Thames. Here a barge waited to take them to the Royal Yacht.

The newly-weds' car was slowed down by well-wishers as they made their way to Battle Bridge Pier, and they were late arriving on board the Royal Yacht Britannia, which was commissioned to take them on a three-month cruise of the Caribbean for their honeymoon.

Princess Margaret wore a buttercup yellow outfit designed by Victor Stiebel.

61

"Fine weather, ceremony and celebration… Exactly on time his bride arrived. Ivory silk taffeta, lace, sequins, pearls and diamonds…The crowd roared with approval as the Prince and Princess of Wales appeared. Bells and flags and banners, cheering and waving, a royal progress through London…"
Kate Adie, BBC, 1981

The Wider Impact

ROYAL WEDDINGS WERE TRADITIONALLY relatively private affairs, attended by the upper echelons of society. The general public hoped to catch a glimpse of the couple on the streets of London, and afterwards they pored over details of the day in illlustrated magazines and newspapers.

Crowds flocked to cinemas to see newsreels of Elizabeth Bowes-Lyon's wedding to the future George VI, but a live radio broadcast was eschewed because Church officials feared that "disrespectful people wearing hats might listen in public houses." During the war the hesitant voice of George VI became a radio fixture, as he broadcast a series of patriotic speeches to the nation. It was inevitable that the marriage of his daughter, Princess Elizabeth, would be broadcast live on radio. A total of 200 million people listened worldwide.

The first ever live televised wedding was the marriage of Princess Margaret to Antony Armstrong-Jones in 1960, which drew an audience of 300 million. The penultimate record-breaker was the wedding of Prince Charles and Lady Diana Spencer in 1981, which drew television audiences of over 750 million worldwide, making it one of the most popular live telecasts of all time.

At Princess Margaret's wedding a CCTV system enabled guests in all parts of the Abbey to see the main ceremony in the sanctuary, while loudspeakers relayed the service to the crowds.

The BBC had located cameras inside the Abbey and along the wedding route and offered a full broadcast of the occasion, ending with the couple's balcony appearance.

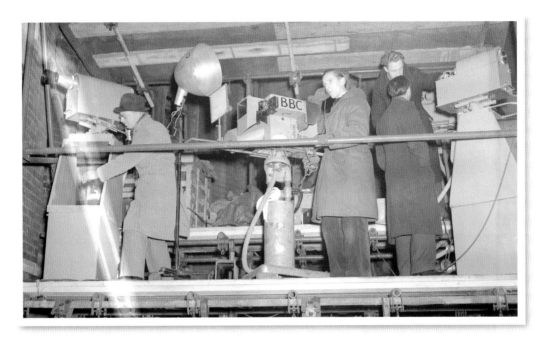

Although the marriage of Princess Elizabeth in 1947 was only broadcast live on the radio, the BBC filmed the procession, service and balcony appearance and highlights were broadcast on television later in the day. The film was broadcast with narration delivered live from the TV studio. This was the first occasion on which cameras were allowed into the Abbey itself. Radio commentators shared the organ loft with the choir.

The marriage of Prince Charles and Lady Diana Spencer on 29 July 1981 saw the arrival of an age of press and media coverage that the royal family had never experienced before. There was worldwide interest in the marriage, with a television audience of 750 million. There was also unprecedented press coverage of the wedding and Diana's image soon became a global commodity. Here, a battery of long lenses are held at the ready as the couple prepare to make the much-anticpated balcony appearance.

William

HRH Prince William Arthur Philip Louis of Wales's entrance into this world on 21 June 1982 set the pioneering style for the years to follow. William was the first heir presumptive to be born in hospital (St. Mary's in West London) and his father, the Prince of Wales, was at his mother's side. Charles's and Diana's desire that their son's upbringing should be 'normal' could only ever be paradoxical; he would always be under intense global scrutiny.

"The one thing his father and I were absolutely agreed on was that William would have as normal an upbringing as possible."
Diana, Princess of Wales

HRH Prince William of Wales

THE LITTLE PRINCE'S CHRISTENING, on 4 August 1982 in Buckingham Palace's imposing music room, was hardly an everyday event. The Archbishop of Canterbury, Dr Robert Runcie, conducted the ceremony and baby Wales wore the traditional christening gown of Honiton lace that had first been worn by Queen Victoria's eldest daughter. His godparents were King Constantine of Greece, Sir Laurens van der Post, Princess Alexandra, the Duchess of Westminster, Lord Romsey and Lady Susan Hussey. Two years later, in 1984, William's younger brother, Prince Harry, was born.

The Prince and Princess of Wales made good their pledge to give their son some of the pleasures of an ordinary childhood. They broke with the royal tradition that consigned children to the nursery by taking William with them on their official tour of Australia and New Zealand in March 1983 when he was less than a year old. Their relaxed parental style was also signalled by his nicknames: Wills and Wombat.

Another royal first came with the Wales's decision to send their son to Mrs Mynor's Nursery School, which was within walking distance of Kensington Palace (William's home for the first 16 years of his life). From there William moved to

Above: School reports from Ludgrove reveal William's sporting talents. He impressed as a rugby and hockey team captain, a crack shot, an excellent football and basketball player, and a school representative at cross-country running and swimming.

Right, top to bottom: William was destined from an early age to follow his forefathers into the armed services, but Diana ensured that he had a normal childhood. He also learnt not to be overshadowed by his illustrious parents.

nearby Wetherby pre-preparatory school. In the past, the children of senior royalty had spent their early years being tutored at home, meaning they were often unaccustomed to socialising with other children. Diana was keen her sons should not miss out on normal childhood treats, such as visits to Disney World, the cinema, go-karting circuits and McDonald's. Later on, Diana took her boys to rugby matches and her populist influence can be seen in William's lifelong support of Aston Villa Football Club. She was once even spotted with the boys queuing alongside other parents to see Santa in Selfridge's. She also ensured her sons got an insight into less privileged lives via her charity work, taking both boys to visit AIDS patients and shelters for the homeless.

In 1990 the eight-year-old Prince started at Ludgrove School in Wokingham, where he first showed his flair for sport and outdoor pursuits, becoming captain of the rugby and hockey teams. The following year he undertook his first public engagement, arriving with his parents at Llandaff Cathedral in Wales with a daffodil pinned to his lapel, to celebrate St. David's Day. It was when William signed the Cathedral's visitors' book that the ever-vigilant press noted he was left-handed. Towards the end of William's first year at prep school a fellow pupil walloped him on the head with a golf club and he had an operation at Great Ormond Street Hospital to correct a depressed fracture of the skull.

Towards the end of 1992, while William was still at Ludgrove, his parents took the decision to separate. This followed a series of public disclosures about their disintegrating relationship. The Princess drove to the school to tell William and Harry the news of the impending separation in person. William, who his mother viewed as the more sensitive of the two brothers, is said to have been distraught. The next few years saw further revelations from both of William's parents, which must have been very hard for a sensitive teenage boy. In 1994 Prince Charles gave a television interview to Jonathan Dimbleby in which he discussed his relationship with Camilla Parker Bowles; a year later Diana was even more candid in her Panorama interview with Martin Bashir.

Prince William and Prince Harry were under intense media scrutiny after their mother's death, but were stoical and dignified in the face of the tragedy and the unprecedented display of public grieving.

The fact that Prince William emerged from this background of public soul-bearing as such a level-headed young man is testament to his natural strength of character and confirms that, despite their rift, both parents were devoted to their sons and always made joint decisions in their best interests.

The autumn of 1995 saw one of the more significant departures from royal precedent when William started his senior school education at Eton, rather than Gordonstoun, where Prince Philip, Prince Charles and his brothers had all been educated. William was far happier at school than his father had been, fitting in well and continuing to excel at sport, becoming 'keeper', or head, of swimming, taking up water polo and captaining his house football team. In the holidays, he acquired his father's fondness for blood sports and polo.

In sixth form, William was elected to Pop, Eton's prefect society, whose members are allowed to wear waistcoats of their own design – the Prince was photographed sporting one fashioned as a Union Jack. It was at Eton that William acquired the easy manners, charm and confidence that are associated with the school, along with its drive for academic excellence.

The House of Windsor has not generally been distinguished by its academic achievements, but William's grades are amongst the best of any modern royal.

Prince William's years at Eton were interrupted in tragic fashion by the news of his mother's death. Diana Princess of Wales was killed in a car crash in Paris in the early hours of 31 August 1997. Prince William and Prince Harry were staying at Balmoral Castle for an annual summer break with their father and grandparents. Prince Charles broke the news to his sons when they woke: William was 15, while Harry was still two weeks away from his 13th birthday.

The Prince was said to be particularly protective of his father in the face of media criticism of the royal family's emotional reticence. A year later, following the unprecedented public grief for the princess and often mawkish press coverage, Prince William and his brother issued a statement asking that mourning should cease. The princes said their mother 'would have known that constant reminders of her death can create nothing but pain to those she left behind.' William took an equally firm line over the many revelatory books published after Diana's death.

Below: The young princes
conducted themselves with
extraordinary dignity at the
funeral, walking behind the
horse-drawn gun carriage
carrying Diana's coffin, alongside
their father, Prince Philip and
Diana's brother Earl Spencer.

William said his mother *"would have known that constant reminders of her death can create nothing but pain to those she left behind."*

When confronted by the revelations that followed her death, he said:
"Harry and I are both quite upset about it, that our mother's trust has been betrayed and that even now she is being exploited."

Below: The young princes conducted themselves with extraordinary dignity at the funeral, walking behind the horse-drawn gun carriage carrying Diana's coffin, alongside their father, Prince Philip and Diana's brother Earl Spencer.

Prince William spent ten weeks working for Operation Raleigh in Chile as part of his gap year. He threw himself into construction projects, taught English, danced salsa with the locals and enjoyed joking and fooling around with the children in the Patagonian village where he was based. His project manager described him as 'very humble and laid back'.

In the spring of 1998 Prince Charles took his two bruised sons on a skiing trip to Whistler in the mountains of British Columbia. According to the press pack who accompanied the princes, as soon as the plane touched down in Vancouver a spontaneous new phenomenon was evident: 'Will Mania'. Wherever the non-plussed Prince went, packs of over-excited teenage girls turned up to mob him, shrieking his name. William had inherited his mother's role as international pin-up, but was understandably reluctant to take up that mantle.

Prince William left Eton in the summer of 2000 with three good A Levels (A in geography, B for History of Art and C in biology) and took a gap year as he pondered his university options. William's 'gap year' seemed expressly designed to foster both a sense of duty and adventure. He joined the Welsh Guards on survival exercises in the humid jungle of Belize before visiting Southern Chile, where he volunteered for a Raleigh International project, teaching schoolchildren and working on construction schemes. There was a somewhat less arduous trip to Mauritius, where he helped with the Royal Geographical Society's marine conservation project and a three-month safari in Africa, where he learned about conservation. Demonstrating a savvy approach to his public image, William later declared that his favourite part of the gap year was when he worked on a dairy farm for £3.20 an hour: "I got my hands dirty, did all the chores and had to get up at 4am."

In September 2001 Prince William enrolled as an undergraduate at the University of St. Andrews, citing the coastal position and Scotland's rolling, wild landscape as a major reason for his choice. He had broken with tradition by rejecting the long-established royal link with Trinity College Cambridge. He elected to read History of Art and to live alongside his fellow students, but arrived just after Fresher's Week, knowing that he could not afford to "end up in a gutter, completely wrecked." Prince Charles and his son had discussed ground rules for his behaviour: no smoking, no drugs, no attempts to slip away from his bodyguard, and no smooching with girls in public. Drinking was sanctioned, but only in moderation. With these provisos, William took up residence in St. Salvator's Hall.

A floor below William, a fellow fresher called Kate Middleton was also settling in. Media myth has it that the Prince's eyes were first opened to Middleton's charms when she strode down the catwalk at a student fashion show in March 2002, wearing a sheer dress that revealed her black underwear. This, however, seems fanciful in light of the fact that William and Kate were both on the same course, reading History of Art, and moved in the same university circles. The fact that by April of that year William, Kate and two friends were house-hunting together for accommodation for their second year demonstrates a far steadier, growing intimacy than one thunder-struck fashion moment. Kate was a sensible confidante, who bolstered the Prince when he had misgivings about St. Andrews at the end of his first year and backed his resolution to switch his course to Geography.

William's second year at university marked a more relaxed time, as the press honoured a pledge to let the Prince study in peace. William said, "I do all my own shopping. I go out, get takeaways, rent videos, go to the cinema, just basically anything I want to really," showing how unusual that prolonged freedom was for a royal heir presumptive.

The Concert for Diana, held at Wembley Stadium in London on 30 June 2007, was, in the words of Prince William "about all that my mother loved in life: her music, her dance, her charities and her family and friends." Guest artists included Diana's favourites, Elton John, Take That, Duran Duran and Tom Jones.

"All these questions about 'Do you want to be King?' It's not a question of wanting to be, it's something I was born into and it's my duty...
It's a very important role and it's one that I don't take lightly."
Prince William

When Prince William was 21, in June 2003, he stepped into the solemn role of Counsellor of State, becoming one of a select few senior royals who has delegated powers to act on behalf of the Queen. Prince Charles held a large, African-themed party for his son at Windsor Castle, where Kate Middleton was one of the guests from St. Andrews. William gave a landmark interview in which he denied having a steady girlfriend and said, "My guiding principles are to be honest, genuine, thoughtful and caring." More telling was his comment, "I'm not an over-dominant person. I don't go around and expect everyone to listen to me the whole time," but he admitted to being "slightly stubborn, because everybody wants you for one reason or another. If you don't stick to your guns and stick to your decision, then you lose control." He exposed a wilder side, confessing his "passion" for high-performance motorbikes and the sense of anonymity afforded by a helmet.

That autumn William, Kate and their two flatmates moved into a country cottage for their third year at St. Andrews. Their intimacy deepened and in March 2004 the couple were photographed together on the ski slopes of Klosters; Clarence House did not deny a royal romance.

Charity prince: Prince William (far left) helps in the kitchen during a visit to a Centrepoint homeless hostel on 20 December 2006. He became patron of the charity, which his mother had also supported, in 2003. In January 2007 (centre) he wears the badge of the Red Cross, joining volunteers in the relief effort for the victims of the South Asian tsunami. In July 2004 (near left) he joins a Fun Run for Sport Relief.

In April Prince William was a witness at Prince Charles's marriage to Camilla Parker Bowles, but the preparations did not impede his studies. On 23rd June he graduated from St. Andrews with a 2:1 in Geography in the presence of the Queen and Prince Charles – the best degree ever gained by a member of the immediate royal family.

Post university, William's life was far more rigorously mapped out than his girlfriend's. The Prince undertook his first official overseas tour, to New Zealand, representing the Queen at events commemorating the 60th anniversary of the end of the Second World War. He then carried out work experience at a leading City bank during the summer, as well as a spell at Chatsworth House in the Peak District, getting some grasp of land management; he also joined a Welsh mountain rescue team for a fortnight.

In October the Prince passed his Regular Commissions Board (a rigorous assessment process) to gain entry to the Royal Military Academy at Sandhurst. Throughout the arduous 44-week course the Prince was known as Officer Cadet Wales and his fellow trainee officers described him warmly as "a normal guy". The Queen showed her respect for her grandson by

appointing William Commodore-in-Chief of Scotland and Commodore-in-Chief of Submarines in August 2006. At the end of that year Prince William passed out of Sandhurst in front of the Queen and an audience that included Prince Charles, Kate Middleton and her parents. William received his commission as a second lieutenant in the Household Cavalry (Blues and Royals) and went on to do four months training in an armoured reconnaissance unit at Bovington Camp in Dorset.

The Prince had always said, "I would want to go where my men went," but his wish to see active service was discouraged by officials. Instead, William went on to train with both the Royal Navy and Royal Air Force, winning a commission as a sub-lieutenant in the former and a flying officer in the latter. William's military commitments meant he was less focused on his girlfriend, leading to strains in the relationship. In April 2007 it was reported that the 24-year-old Prince had split from Kate Middleton.

William had other pressing concerns at the time, including Harry's and his ambitious plan to stage a concert to mark the tenth anniversary of their mother's death.

Prince William, Flt Lt William Wales, flies a Griffin helicopter with 60 Squadron Defence Helicopter Flying school at RAF Shawbury on 18 June 2009. After graduating from RAF Shawbury in 2010 he was given further training on Sea Kings at RAF Valley on Anglesey.

"My whole heart was in the Army. That's why I joined them and I did everything, as much as could be done. It's just a pity I couldn't get to Afghanistan. I still have hope and faith and real determination to get out there."
Prince William

The Concert for Diana was held on 1 July 2007, which would have been Diana's 46th birthday. The Princes hosted the event with aplomb; it was broadcast to 140 countries, with proceeds going to select charities. Kate Middleton's presence in the Royal Box was noted, even though she kept a decorous distance from William. At the after-party, however, the estranged couple were more intimate and within months Kate was back in the royal fold.

In January 2008 William started an intensive four-month pilot training course with the Royal Air Force at Cranwell. It was later revealed that during this secondment the Prince had flown to Afghanistan as part of a mission to repatriate the body of a fallen soldier, Trooper Robert Pearson. Prince Charles presented his son with his RAF wings in April 2008 and on 17th June William received an even more distinguished honour when the Queen installed her grandson as a Royal Knight Companion of the Most Noble Order of the Garter at Windsor Chapel. Prince William transferred his commission from the army to the RAF in January 2009 and was promoted to Flight Lieutenant. He then began training to become a 'search and rescue' helicopter pilot, graduating from the flying school at RAF

Shawbury in 2010 before moving to RAF Valley on Anglesey, where he was assigned to No. 22 Squadron for further training on Sea Kings. In September he graduated and began service as a co-pilot. He moved, with Kate, to a cottage in Anglesey, becoming the first British heir presumptive to live openly with a girlfriend. In February 2011, the Queen approved the appointment of Prince William as Colonel of the Irish Guards, marking Prince William's first honorary appointment in the Army, and the Irish Guards' first Royal Colonel.

To further their charitable work, Prince William and Prince Harry created their own Foundation in 2009 which focuses on issues that they both care about: helping young people in society; raising awareness and support for servicemen and women; and developing sustainable models of living in the light of climate change and dwindling natural resources.

Charles's and Diana's desire that their firstborn should have some sense of normality, despite his royal heritage, has paid rich dividends. William is a thoroughly modern prince, whose diligence, modesty and ability to communicate warmly with everyone who crosses his path are undisputed.

Grandmother's inspection: The Queen glances up at Prince William as she inspects the cadets at The Royal Military Academy during the Sovereign's Parade in Camberley, 15 December 2006. Prince William was among the 446 officer cadets on parade; of this number, 227 passed out receiving their commission and becoming officers. He went on to to join the Household Cavalry (Blues and Royals).

Naval Training: Prince William at the Britannia Royal Naval college in Dartmouth, 2008. He spent two months with the Royal Navy following his completion of training with the Royal Air Force. The attachment was designed to familiarise him with the working conditions of the Royal Navy. He took part in operations in the Caribbean on HMS Iron Duke. His military commitments led to a short-lived estrangement from Kate.

Catherine

Catherine Elizabeth Middleton appears to have stood out from the crowd all her life, yet without a hint of ostentation. Her quiet poise undoubtedly finds its roots in her happy and stable upbringing, and in the support and intimacy of her family. As Prince William said fondly of the Middletons in the interview that marked the couple's engagement, "She's got a very, very close family." That affection and loyalty is clearly something the Prince admires.

Kate nostalgically recalled her mother's talent for making parties magical, saying one of her fondest childhood memories was
"the amazing white rabbit marshmallow cake Mummy made me when I was seven."

Catherine Middleton

MICHAEL AND CAROLE MIDDLETON met when they both worked at British Airways (she as an air hostess, he as a flight dispatcher) and soon after their 1980 marriage they moved from a flat in Slough to a modest house in the Berkshire village of Bradfield Southend. Catherine (mostly known as Kate) was the couple's first child and was born on 9 January 1982 at the Royal Berkshire Hospital. The Middletons had their daughter christened in June at the local church of St. Andrew's. In September 1983 Kate's sister Pippa was born and eight months later Michael Middleton was posted to Jordan with BA, where the family lived until Kate was four.

In the autumn of 1986 the Middletons returned to their Berkshire home and Kate started at Bradfield Church of England Primary School. The following April Kate's brother James was born. The expanded family were, by all accounts, active in village life, using the local toddler group and pre-school and attending church fairs, while both sisters became enthusiastic members of the 1st St. Andrew's Brownie pack.

James's arrival coincided with Carole's decision to start a business selling children's party bags, games and decorations to time-pressed parents. The business thrived and by the

Above: At St. Andrew's Prep School, Kate excelled at sport, spending many Saturdays playing netball and hockey, while she went skiing in the school holidays. She also won swimming races and broke the school record for her age group at high jump. A contemporary, Samantha Garland, later recalled, "I don't think there was a sport that she couldn't turn her hand to."

Kate and her younger sister Pippa, with their father, enjoying the ancient ruins of Jordan. He was posted there by British Airways in 1984, when Kate was just two years old, and the family stayed there until she was four.

time Kate was seven her parents could afford to send her to a private co-educational preparatory school, St. Andrew's School in Pangbourne, West Berkshire.

At St. Andrew's Kate excelled at sport, learnt ballet and tap-dancing and was keen on drama, playing Eliza at the age of ten in a school production of *My Fair Lady*. Kate's final school performance, in a production of the Victorian melodrama *Murder in the Red Barn*, seemed altogether more prescient. Kate played an innocent young woman, courted by a rich young man, coincidentally called William. Early in the play a fortune-telling gypsy declares, "Soon you will meet a handsome man, a rich gentleman." Miss Middleton's character replies, "It is all I have ever hoped for". The gypsy then foretells she will be married and taken away to London, at which the young actress sighs, "Oh how my heart flutters!"

Carole and Michael Middleton identified the business potential of the internet early on, which aided Party Pieces' already rapid expansion. In 1995 the company moved to larger business premises and the Middletons upgraded too, to a spacious five-bedroom house on the outskirts of the pretty Berkshire village of Chapel Row. In September 1995 Kate

moved to Downe House School, an all-girls boarding school in Berkshire, where she did not thrive. Friends later said she was bullied and it has been noted that one of the charities Kate and William have nominated for donations, in lieu of a wedding list, is called Beatbullying.

In April 1996 Kate's concerned parents moved her to the co-educational Marlborough College in Wiltshire (alumni include Samantha Cameron and Princess Eugenie), where she blossomed. The girl who one former classmate at St. Andrew's, Kingsley Glover, described as "shy, skinny and lanky" was transformed into a confident and attractive young woman. A former schoolmaster said, "She was universally liked and, to top it all, she was a joy to teach." Kate shone academically, gaining eleven GCSEs and three A Levels (in Art, Biology and Chemistry), gained her Duke of Edinburgh's Gold Award, and continued to excel at sport, representing the school at tennis, hockey, netball and athletics. Contemporaries recalled a good fun, yet naturally decorous pupil, who didn't have to step out of line to be popular.

There was never the slightest whiff of rebellion. Her former classmate Jessica Hay said in a newspaper interview, "I never

"I went bright red and scuttled off."
Kate Middleton on being introduced
to Prince William

once saw her drunk. Even after our GCSEs, she only drank a couple of glugs of vodka." Even the famous story of Kate having a picture of Prince William pinned to her school bedroom wall appears to be a myth. In the October 2010 interview with Tom Bradby that marked the royal engagement Kate said very firmly that she had the "Levi's guy on my wall, not a picture of William." Although Jessica Hay claims Kate once said of the young Prince, "I bet he's kind. You can tell just by looking at him".

In 2000 Kate Middleton took a gap year. She headed to Florence in September for an intensive 12-week course in Italian at the British Institute. Once again, Kate's fellow students related that she was fun, but exercised natural self-restraint; she didn't get drunk, didn't smoke and certainly didn't experiment with drugs, yet wasn't judgmental about others' excesses. Coincidentally Kate, like William, went to Chile on a Raleigh International Programme. There was also a family holiday in Barbados and a stint crewing Round the World Challenge boats in the Solent.

In 2001 Kate enrolled at St. Andrews University to read History of Art and moved into St. Salvator's Hall of residence, alongside Prince William. The pair soon became good friends, mixing with the same crowd and recognising a shared passion for outdoor pursuits. William also cited her "really naughty sense of humour", as a big draw. A fellow student, Laura Warshauer, has told how the pair attended a Harry Potter themed ball at St. Andrew's Castle in the November of their first term, where William 'bought' Kate, who was dressed as a schoolgirl, at a charity slave auction. Warshauer also recounted how Kate rescued William from a persistent admirer at a party by walking up and putting her arms around him, while William told his pursuer, "I'm sorry, I have a girlfriend." The Prince then mouthed, "Thank you!", to Kate. Nevertheless, Kate's first boyfriend at St. Andrews was law student Rupert Finch.

Kate first caught the media's attention when she modelled in a student fashion show in March 2002, for which William had bought a £200 front row seat. Kate threw herself into university life, becoming a founder member

Country girl: Kate Middleton wears tweed at the Game Fair, Blenheim Palace, 2004. Aged 22, Kate worked as a model for the Really Wild Clothing Company, a business based at the Royal Berkshire Shooting School. Kate appeared in their 2004 catalogue and also modelled the clothing in person at the 2004 Game Fair.

of the all-female Lumsden Club (set up to rival the men-only Kate Kennedy Club, which William eventually joined), named after a 19th-century Scottish educationalist. Like most students, Kate had to supplement her student income with part time work. She waited tables briefly in one St. Andrews café and had a holiday job at the end of her first year serving drinks at Henley Regatta for an upmarket catering service.

In September 2002 Kate Middleton moved into a flat in St. Andrews with Prince William and two mutual friends. In May the following year the couple were photographed deep in conversation at a rugby match; but at the time of his 21st birthday in June the Prince denied he had a serious girlfriend. Kate and William attended each other's 21st birthday parties and, in September 2003, the flatmates found new lodgings in a cottage on a picturesque farm outside St. Andrews and it's believed the romance started around Christmas. The relationship was only confirmed, however, when William and Kate were photographed together on the ski slopes of Klosters in March 2004. However Kate did not attend Prince Charles's marriage to Camilla Parker Bowles in the spring of 2005 – although she did attend the June wedding of Hugh van Cutsem, one of William's closest friends.

Far left: William and Kate are keen skiers. When they were photographed at Klosters in 2004 William told a reporter that he was too young to get married.

Left: Kate Middleton leaves her Chelsea home in 2007 pursued by photographers. In January 2010 her solicitors acted against a paparazzi who had taken photos of her family. The matter was settled with a warning.

Kate graduated from St. Andrews on 23 June 2005 with a 2:1 in the History of Art. The Middletons were there to applaud her, but they didn't mingle with Prince William's royal family party. Kate's path after university was less clear than William's. She faced the hurdles of any Arts graduate looking for a job, but was further constrained by her relationship with the highest-profile young male in the country. Elements of the press dubbed Kate 'Waity Katy' and characterised her as a workshy socialite, but for the greatest part of the years leading to Kate's engagement she worked for her parent's company; Party Pieces afforded her flexibility and, crucially, guaranteed discretion.

In October 2005 a newspaper published a paparazzi photograph of Kate Middleton gazing from the top floor of a London bus. She engaged Prince Charles's media lawyers, Harbottle and Lewis, who wrote to newspaper and magazine editors, asking them to respect her privacy. The following February it was suggested Kate might receive her own security detail, prompting rumours of an engagement. The retail chain Woolworths even started to manufacture souvenirs. 2006 was also the year that Kate first featured on a style icon list, when the *Daily Telegraph* made her their 'Most Promising Newcomer.'

Over the next few years her increasingly chic, if conservative, dress sense would be hailed by other style arbiters, including *Tatler, People* magazine and *Vanity Fair*.

Kate's relaxed air with William's intimate family circle was noted when, in March 2006, she appeared on the balcony of the Royal Box at the Cheltenham Gold Cup, alongside Charles and Camilla. Later that year Prince William extended his intimacy with Kate's family, when the young couple took a summer holiday on Ibiza with her uncle Gary Goldsmith, who owns an impressive villa on the island; but the wisdom of the visit was called into question afterwards, when a tabloid sting exposed Gary Goldsmith's drug use and louche lifestyle. It is, to date, the only time a whiff of scandal has touched the impeccably discreet Middleton clan.

Kate started work in November for the women's fashion chain, Jigsaw, as an accessories buyer. The firm's co-founder, Belle Robinson, later said, "I was so impressed by her." Robinson described how Kate "sat in the kitchen at lunchtime and chatted with everyone from the van drivers to the accounts girls." In December 2006 Kate and her parents were the guests of Prince William at Sandhurst

In September 2008 Kate helped to organise the charity fund-raising 'Day-Glo Midnight Roller Disco'. Looking glamorous in eye-catching fancy dress, she was also snapped while sprawled on the floor after taking a tumble on roller skates.

Military Academy when he passed out as an army officer in the presence of the Queen. Lip-reading experts claimed that Kate, looking glamorous in a Philip Treacy hat, exclaimed at one point, "I love the uniform, it's so sexy!".

In January 2007 News International and the Guardian Media Group agreed to stop using paparazzi pictures of Kate in response to a plea from Prince William for media harassment of his girlfriend to cease. Former Royal Press Secretary Dickie Arbiter compared the press interest to the frenzied pursuit of Diana. There were other strains on the relationship, as the Prince concentrated on his military career and, following heartfelt talks during a spring skiing holiday, Kate and William agreed to split.

Kate later said to Tom Bradby of the decision, "I wasn't very happy about it, but actually it made me a stronger person. You find out things about yourself that maybe you hadn't realised. I think you can get quite consumed by a relationship when you're younger." Kate's public demeanour continued to be cheerful and dignified, despite press reporting of cruel comments – allegedly made by members of William's circle – that disparaged the Middleton family's social standing. She was

Kate Middleton stands at the helm of a Chinese dragon boat, part of the Sisterhood, a team of charity fund-raising athletes who planned to cross the Channel in 2007. Security concerns about her involvement forced her to stand down.

A friend supposedly said to Kate, "You're so lucky to be going out with William!" to which she is said to have replied "He's so lucky to be going out with me."

seen at Badminton Horse Trials and joined the Sisterhood, a fund-raising team of female athletes, who were training to cross the Channel in a Chinese Dragon boat.

That June William and Harry staged their memorial concert for Diana at Wembley Stadium and it was noted that an enthusiastic Kate was amongst the guests in the Royal Box. In October she was photographed with Prince Charles at Balmoral as she was taught to use a bolt-action hunting rifle, before joining a deer stalking party. The photos signalled Kate and William were firmly back on track. A month later Kate left her job at Jigsaw and returned to her flexible working arrangement with her parent's company.

In April 2008 Kate was watching as Prince Charles presented William with his wings at RAF Cranwell, while in May she represented her boyfriend at Peter Phillips's marriage to Autumn Kelly; it was there she was formally introduced to the Queen for the first time. In June Kate joined the royal family group at Windsor Chapel watching William installed as a Knight of the Garter. It was the first time Kate had attended an official royal public occasion, and she and Harry were observed laughing uproariously at William in his

ceremonial robes and feather-plumed hat. For the next two years the royal romance was conducted steadily, but largely stealthily – the couple were rarely photographed together.

When Prince William transferred to RAF Valley in 2010 for his training on Sea Kings, Kate started spending an increasing amount of time with him in Wales, quietly becoming the first such prominent royal bride-to-be to cohabit before her wedding. In October 2010 William took Kate to Lewa Wildlife Park in Kenya, and proposed to her in a lodge nestling in the Mount Kenya range, close to Lake Alice. The wedding was announced on 16 November 2010.

The Palace announcement used the more formal 'Catherine', and from this point on Kate was transformed into princess-in-waiting, Catherine Middleton. She had persuaded William that she was not only willing to tailor her life to the man she loved, she was ideally suited to the role of royal consort with her innate poise, grace, intelligence and discretion.

Self-composed Catherine is respectful, but not over-awed, in the face of royalty. And, the truth remains: Prince William and the royal family are lucky to have her.

When Prince William proposed to Kate in Kenya he offered her his mother, Diana's, sapphire and diamond engagement ring – which, he said later, he had kept in a rucksack for the duration of their holiday. On their return William asked Kate's father, Michael, for his permission to marry Kate, although the announcement was delayed due to the death of her paternal grandfather. Kate gave her first media interview, alongside Prince William, to ITV News's Tom Bradby. She sounded a little nervous, but looked spectacular in a royal blue Issa dress, which became instantly iconic and spawned a thousand imitations. She told Tom Bradby that William's proposal had been "*very* romantic."

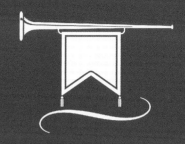

The Wedding Day

Rain had been forecast all week, but Friday 29th April was fated to be a day of small miracles and untrammelled joy. From 5am, first a trickle, then a swelling torrent of people flooded towards Westminster, as London awoke to the world's gaze. Not for a generation had the British nation given itself to such a show of pageantry and jubilation. Catherine Middleton, the descendant of Durham miners and Leeds lawyers, was marrying her Prince. This was history in the making.

In 2006 restorers removed centuries of dirt and grime from the beautiful Cosmati Pavement, in front of the High Altar, which was created in the 13th century. It is made up of rare marbles and gemstones and pieces of coloured glass, set in complex allegorical patterns into a framework of Purbeck marble.

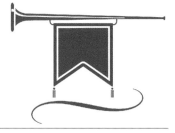

Westminster Abbey

THE ABBEY OWES ITS ORIGINS to King Edgar (reigned 959–75), who first gave a community of Benedictine monks substantial lands covering much of the West End of London. The Gothic building, which still stands today, was built in the mid-13th century by Henry III around the shrine of the Anglo-Saxon saint, Edward the Confessor, who is buried there.

Inspiration was taken from the Gothic cathedrals of Reims, Amiens and Chartres, with their pointed arches, ribbed vaulting, rose windows and flying buttresses. In fact the Abbey has the highest Gothic vault in England (103 ft), and the narrowness of the aisle makes it appear even more lofty. It is richly endowed with stained glass, paintings, textiles, decorated marble pavements, monumental sculpture and memorials. It is the place where some of the most important people in the nation's history are buried or commemorated.

Westminster Abbey is a 'royal peculiar', a concept dating back to Anglo-Saxon times whereby a church finds itself under the personal jurisdiction of the sovereign rather than a bishop. The only people that can be married in the Abbey are members of the royal family, Order of the Bath members and their children, and anyone living in the Abbey's precincts.

Westminster Abbey has been the setting for 38 coronations, starting with William the Conqueror in 1066. Up until this point, coronations had taken place at various locations – Bath, Winchester, Canterbury. William's predecessor, Harold Godwineson, may also have been crowned at Westminster, though there is no documentary evidence. The Coronation Chair, ordered by Edward I in 1298, has been used at every coronation. The Abbey is the last resting place of 17 monarchs; the last monarch to be buried there was George II in 1760. The funerals of the Queen Mother and Princess Diana were held there, but neither was buried at the Abbey.

The first royal wedding at the Abbey was in 1100, when Henry I wed Matilda of Scotland. From 1382 to 1919 no royal marriages were held at the Abbey; the tradition was revived when Victoria's granddaughter, Patricia of Connaught, chose it for her wedding to Alexander Ramsay.

William has followed in the footsteps of his grandparents, Princess Elizabeth and Philip Mountbatten, and also his great-grandparents Albert (later George VI) and Elizabeth Bowes-Lyon, who exchanged their wedding vows at the Abbey's magnificent High Altar.

Catherine Middleton's florist Shane Connolly decorated the Abbey on 29th April. The flowers and plants included azaleas, rhododendrons, euphorbias, beeches, wisteria and lilacs. Most striking of all were eight 20 feet-high trees: six English field maple and two hornbeam. The English field maple symbolises humility and reserve, and was used to make loving cups in medieval times, while the hornbeam signifies resilience. The trees also evoked Catherine's family home in Bucklebury, which stands on a historic avenue of oaks.

ROYAL WEDDINGS AT THE ABBEY

11 November 1100:
King Henry I of England was married to Matilda of Scotland

9 April 1269:
Edmund of Crouchback, 1st Earl of Leicester and Lancaster, son of King Henry III was married to Lady Aveline de Forz

30 April 1290:
Joan of Acre, daughter of King Edward I, was married to the 7th Earl of Gloucester

8 July 1290:
Margaret of England, daughter of King Edward I, was married to John II, son of Duke of Brabant

20 January 1382:
King Richard II of England was married to Anne of Bohemia

27 February 1919:
Princess Patricia of Connaught was married to Commander Alexander Ramsay

28 February 1922:
Princess Mary was married to Viscount Lascelles

26 April 1923:
Prince Albert, Duke of York, was married to Lady Elizabeth Bowes-Lyon

29 November 1934:
Prince George, Duke of Kent, was married to Princess Marina of Greece and Denmark

20 November 1947:
Princess Elizabeth (later Queen Elizabeth II), was married to Lieutenant Philip Mountbatten RN (later Duke of Edinburgh)

6 May 1960:
Princess Margaret was married to Antony Armstrong-Jones

24 April 1963:
Princess Alexandra of Kent was married to Angus Ogilvy

14 November 1973:
Princess Anne was married to Lieutenant Mark Phillips

23 July 1986:
Prince Andrew, Duke of York, was married to Miss Sarah Ferguson

29 April 2011:
Prince William of Wales was married to Miss Catherine Middleton

"The colour of the Queen's hat has been the most popular bet to date, with most punters in the yellow camp."
Alex Donohue, Ladbrokes

Arriving at the Abbey

THE EXPECTANT CROWDS, rapt outside Westminster Abbey's West Door, had waited patiently for the wedding day's most exalted players. Some had even slept there. William and Catherine were sensitive to Britain's recent economic downturn, ruling against unnecessary pomp for the procession to the Abbey. Instead of the customary horse-drawn carriages, cars from the Royal Fleet were used, while foreign royals and less senior members of the British royal family travelled in a fleet of minibuses looking, as one wag said, "like tourists on a day trip to Blackpool".

Prince William and Prince Harry were the first of the main wedding party to arrive, at just after 10.15am. Each arrival was timed with military precision and accompanied by a police security detail. The Queen and most of the royal family left from Buckingham Palace, but Prince William and Prince Harry, followed by Prince Charles and the Duchess of Cornwall, departed from Clarence House. The Middletons made their journey into the history books from the Goring Hotel, with the bride and her father the last to arrive, stepping on to the red carpet from a romantic Rolls Royce Phantom VI. As Catherine Middleton paused to wave on the red carpet she looked every inch the princess.

Left: The Dean of Westminster in his gold ceremonial robes greets Her Majesty the Queen as she arrives at the Abbey, after making the five-minute journey from Buckingham Palace. As she entered through the West Door she was hailed by a fanfare from the State Trumpeters of the Household Cavalry, before greeting Prince Charles and the Duchess of Cornwall, the Archbishop of Canterbury and the Bishop of London.

Below: Catherine Middleton arrives and greets the wildly cheering crowds, while her sister, and maid of honour, Pippa gathers up her train so that their father, Michael, can escort his daughter into the Abbey. The bride's silk tulle veil remained over her face until she reached the High Altar; then her father Michael lifted it gently over her head to reveal the 'Halo' tiara, loaned by the Queen.

"In a sense every wedding is a royal wedding with the bride and groom as King and Queen of creation, making a new life together, so that life can flow through them into the future."
The Bishop of London

Leading Roles

THERE WERE THORNY ISSUES of protocol concerning which leading Anglican clergyman should preside over which part of the service. The Dean of Westminster, the Very Reverend Dr John Hall, clearly had to have a central role, as he was effectively hosting the event. However, the marriage of an heir to the throne calls for the participation of the Church of England's Primate, the Archbishop of Canterbury, the Most Reverend Dr Rowan Williams. Then there was the royal confidante, the Bishop of London, the Right Reverend Dr Richard Chartres, to consider. Chartres was a trustee of Princess Diana's will and confirmed both Prince William and Catherine Middleton (Catherine's confirmation happened shortly before her wedding). William and Catherine found a diplomatic solution by asking the Dean to conduct the actual service, the Archbishop to solemnise the marriage vows, and the Bishop to give the Address.

The Dean's clear, warm and refreshingly unflashy delivery set the intimate tone of a parish wedding as he declaimed the familiar introduction to the marriage service: "Dearly beloved, we are gathered here in the sight of God… to join together this man and woman in Holy Matrimony." Next the Archbishop of Canterbury, in his effulgent crimson and gold ceremonial robes, took the Dean's place at the High Altar to officiate over the wedding vows. Rowan Williams looked every inch the poet, scholar and man of scrupulous conscience that he is. Some sonorous voices seem designed for great events: so it is with the Archbishop, whose Shakespearean delivery thrilled millions worldwide.

The imposing Bishop of London has a similarly resonant voice. His seven-minute address, delivered from the Abbey's pulpit, was a superbly-pitched clarion call, rallying the faithful to recognise the spiritual foundations of matrimony and support the young couple. In the opening words he quoted St. Catherine of Siena, whose feast day it was: "Be who God meant you to be and you will set the world on fire."

However, the highest plaudits should, perhaps, be awarded to the wedding service's fourth distinct voice: that of James Middleton. The bride's dyslexic brother, who has no experience performing to vast audiences, delivered the Lesson from Romans 12 with great clarity and a genuine sense of the occasion's majesty. His part in proceedings underlined the fact that Catherine Middleton is not just a remarkable young woman – she is the product of a quite remarkable family.

Far left: A poised James Middleton impresses the congregation at Westminster Abbey with his dignified reading of the lesson. The bride's brother left university after a year to put his energies into establishing his own business, the Cake Kit Company, drawing inspiration from his parents' entrepreneurialism. Friends say they expect him to become "the next Richard Branson".

Left: The Archbishop of Canterbury, in his scarlet and gold mitre, shares a private moment with the Bishop of London (in white vestments) and the gold-robed Dean of Westminster. The three leading clergymen all worked closely with William and Catherine, and one another, to ensure that the spiritual core of the marriage service was never overwhelmed by the grandeur of a great state event.

> *"The ceremony is going to be, without a doubt, the most emotionally intense and exhilarating hour of my life."*
> Paul Mealor, composer

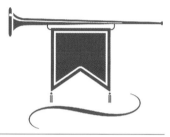

The Music

THE INSPIRED CHOICE OF MUSIC at Westminster Abbey was, for many, the most transporting element of day. Catherine and William put "considerable thought" into every aspect of the selection, which showcased British composers and performers and the musical tradition of the Church of England. The influence of the Prince of Wales was also very evident; a palace spokesman said the bride made some decisions while listening to an iPod alongside her future father-in-law and that Catherine was keen that the Tudor melody *Greensleeves* should be included.

Prominence was given to the work of Charles Hubert Hastings Parry, whose soaring anthem "I Was Glad" was chosen as the Introit for the bride's procession down the Abbey's nave. Parry composed the music for Edward VII's coronation in 1902, and it has been performed at subsequent great state occasions, including the Queen's coronation and Prince Charles' own wedding to Diana Spencer. Parry's March, from his Suite for Aristophanes's *The Birds*, announced the arrival of the Queen, while his much loved musical setting for William Blake's poem *Jerusalem* was chosen as one of the three hymns; the composer's *Blest Pair of Sirens* signalled the service's end.

The service's stirring opening hymn *Guide Me, O Thou Great Redeemer* was an echo from the funeral of Diana Princess of Wales, and the middle hymn, *Love Divine, All Loves Excelling* placed devotion at the heart of the ceremony.

There was a skilful blend of the traditional and modern throughout. Music by Edward Elgar, Benjamin Britten and Ralph Vaughan Williams was played alongside new works, such as young Welsh composer Paul Mealor's spare and contemplative *Ubi Caritas et Amor*. Mealor lives on Anglesey, where the royal couple are also based. The Dean and Chapter of Westminster Abbey commissioned John Rutter to create the playful Anthem *This is the Day* as a wedding present for the bride and groom.

Prince William's air force service was movingly reflected in the third special composition, *Valiant and Brave* (after the motto of No. 22 Squadron – Search and Rescue Helicopters). This piece was composed by Wing Commander Duncan Stubbs and performed by the fanfare team of The Central Band of the RAF. The spine-tingling fanfares by the State Trumpeters of the Household Cavalry also reflected the royal family's close links to the armed forces.

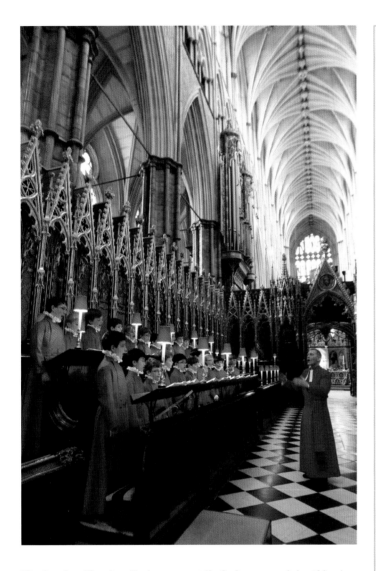

The London Chamber Orchestra and organist Robert Quinney anchored proceedings with flawless performances, while the radiant singing of the choirs of Westminster Abbey and the Chapel Royal moved many to tears. The world-famous Choir of Westminster Abbey (shown practising for the big day) comprises some 30 boys (all of whom attend the Abbey's dedicated residential choir school) and 12 professional adult singers (Lay Vicars). James O'Donnell, the organist and Master of the Choristers, took up his present position in 2000. He is responsible for the Choir's everyday music as well as the many national occasions that take place at the Abbey.

Before the Service
For Organ:
Fantasia in G by Johann Sebastian Bach
Veni Creator Spiritus by the Master of The Queen's Music,
Sir Peter Maxwell Davies
Prelude on St. Columba, Op. 28 by Sir Charles Villiers Stanford
Sonata for Organ, Op. 28 by Edward Elgar

For Orchestra:
Serenade for Strings in E minor by Edward Elgar
Courtly Dance V: Galliard from *Gloriana* by Benjamin Britten
Fantasia on Greensleeves by Ralph Vaughan Williams
Farewell to Stromness by Sir Peter Maxwell Davies
On Hearing the First Cuckoo in Spring by Frederick Delius
Touch Her Soft Lips and Part from *Henry V* Suite
by William Walton
Romance for String Orchestra by Gerald Finzi
Canzona from Organ Sonata in C minor by Percy Whitlock

Processional Music
March from *The Birds* by Sir Charles Hubert Hastings Parry
Prelude on Rhosymedre by Ralph Vaughan Williams
'I Was Glad' by Sir Charles Hubert Hastings Parry

Hymns
'Guide Me, O Thou Great Redeemer',
'Love Divine All Love Excelling'
'Jerusalem'

Choral Music
'This is the Day which the Lord hath made', by John Rutter
Motet *'Ubi caritas'* by Paul Mealor
'Blest Pair of Sirens', from *At a Solemn Musick*,
by Sir Charles Hubert Hastings Parry

Recessional
Crown Imperial by William Walton

After the Service
Toccata from Symphonie V by Charles-Marie Widor and
Pomp and Circumstance March No. 5 by Edward Elgar

> *"William and Catherine are making this commitment very much in the public eye…They will need the support, the solidarity and the prayers of all those who are watching."*
> The Archbishop of Canterbury

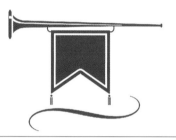

Wedding Vows

THE PRAYER, composed by William and Catherine

God our Father, we thank you for our families, for the love that we share and for the joy of our marriage.

In the busyness of each day keep our eyes fixed on what is real and important in life and help us to be generous with our time and love and energy.

Strengthened by our union, help us to serve and comfort those who suffer. We ask this in the Spirit of Jesus Christ.
Amen.

THE TRADITIONAL VERSION of the Anglican marriage service seems precisely engineered for moments of high drama – and never more so than at the pageant of a royal wedding. When the Archbishop of Canterbury asked, "if either of you know any impediment, why ye may not be lawfully joined together in Matrimony, ye do now confess it," the vast theatre of Westminster Abbey contracted to one intimate stage: the High Altar. The two key players were so rapt in their vows that television viewers had a keen sense of intrusion.

As the Archbishop led the pair through their vows it was clear they spoke the words solely for one another and had become oblivious of the attentive onlookers. Prince William and Catherine Middleton radiated serene certainty. When William was asked if he would, "keep thee only unto her, so long as ye both shall live", his forthright declaration of "I will" prompted a crescendo of cheers from the crowds. Catherine's shyer pledge roused the same enthusiasm.

Rowan Williams presided over the marriage vows with great care and delicacy, steering each participant in their historic role. The poetry of the language, taken from the Series One of the 1966 Book of Common Prayer, added gravitas to proceedings; although, in line with most modern brides, Catherine chose not to "obey" her new husband. William declined to wear a wedding ring – he clearly felt he had no need for a symbolic sign of his devotion.

When Rowan Williams finally linked the bride's and groom's right hands and declared, "Those whom God hath joined together let no man put asunder", the crowds outside the Abbey erupted. Catherine had landed her Prince and everyone agreed he was lucky to have her.

"'It was amazing."
Queen Elizabeth II

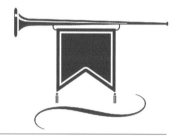

The Return to Buckingham Palace

IF THE JOURNEY TO WESTMINSTER ABBEY had been all modest restraint, the return to the Palace was pure unfettered jubilation. Gone were the cars that had transported the bride, groom and guests to the Abbey and in their place, at last, the great state carriages from the Royal Mews drawn by the Queen's beloved Windsor Greys and Bays.

The 1902 State Landau drew up before the Abbey's Great West Door and the new Duke of Cambridge helped his Duchess into the open carriage, before settling at her side. The procession was headed by mounted police, followed by a Captain's Escort of the Household Cavalry in their ceremonial uniforms, commanded by William's great friend Nicholas van Cutsem, a major in the Life Guards (and uncle of little bridesmaid Grace). Anyone standing on the wedding route could hear the thrilling far-off clatter of hooves, harness, metal breast-plates and carriage wheels, signalling the newly-weds were on their way. A smiling Catherine asked William if he was happy, "Yes! Yes!" he replied.

The couple appeared amazed and gratified by the crowd's size and euphoric support; Catherine's wave became more regal on the return journey, as she mirrored the Prince's gestures.

Their carriage swept down Whitehall, through Horse Guards Parade and then along into the Mall. It was followed by two Ascot Landaus carrying Prince Harry, Pippa Middleton and the pageboys and bridesmaids. Then came a Sovereign's Escort of the Household Cavalry, heralding the procession of the Queen, who travelled in a Semi-State Landau with the Duke of Edinburgh. The applause was just as deafening for the 85-year-old monarch as for bride and groom. Behind the Queen, in the second Semi-State Landau were Prince Charles and the Duchess of Cornwall, united as proud in-laws with Michael and Carole Middleton. Finally came another division of the Sovereign's Escort, their pounding hooves creating a sense of excitement and anticipation in the cheering crowd.

At the procession's head the 1902 State Landau slowed to enter Buckingham Palace's great quadrangle, the horses' hooves echoing. In the only visible hitch of the day, a Palace coachman was flummoxed by the task of helping Catherine from the carriage with her billowing gown. William stepped in and helped his bride arrange herself. When the Queen arrived and ascended the red-carpeted steps of the Grand Entrance to greet her grandson she placed her seal of approval on the day: "It was amazing", she declared.

"We know the world will be watching on April 29th, and the couple are very, very keen indeed that the spectacle should be a classic example of what Britain does best."
Jamie Lowther-Pinkerton,
Private Secretary to Prince William

Pomp and Circumstance

THE BRITISH CHARACTER is too reticent for carnival, instead it excels at pomp and pageantry. On the wedding day of the heir presumptive the country drew on its great treasury of ritual. In Westminster Abbey the Sovereign's Body Guard of the Yeoman Guard Extraordinary, better known as Beefeaters, guarded the aisle. They wore ceremonial garb that has barely altered since Tudor times and their glory was only rivalled by the Archbishop's robes.

More than a thousand military personnel lined the wedding route, drawn from all three services and dressed in every degree of ceremonial splendour. There were guards in their bearskins, Household Cavalry in their plumed helmets, and naval ratings in jaunty white caps. The gleaming brass of six military bands stirred the crowds, and the RAF's Battle of Britain Memorial Flight fly-past was a stirring climax to the ceremonial part of the day. Eighty cadets from the Combined Cadet Force and sixty Explorer Scouts sold official programmes to the crowd.

From the magnificent horse-drawn state carriages to the Union flags that fluttered in The Mall, London was *en fête*. But the greatest pageant of all was the flag-bearing public.

Above: The Prince of Wales and the Duchess of Cornwall, and Michael and Carole Middleton, return to Buckingham Palace in a Semi-State Landau from the Royal Mews with two liveried footmen. This style of carriage was also used for the Investiture of the Prince of Wales at Caernarfon Castle in 1969 and they are also used to transport new Ambassadors and High Commissioners when they are received by the Queen.

Left: The Band of the Scots Guards, which played on Horse Guards Parade. Six military bands entertained the crowds at various points along the wedding route, mixing traditional marching music with more exotic melodies. The Band of the Grenadier Guards delighted people on The Mall with renditions of the Hawaii Five-0 theme tune and Barry Manilow's *Copacabana*.

Left: The Band of the Coldstream Guards march from Buckingham Palace to the Duke of York steps. They played for three hours on the wedding morning and cheered the waiting throng with patriotic favourites, show-tunes and what their director of music, Lieutenant Colonel Graham Jones, called "sing-along stuff". The band is globally renowned and has recorded two best selling albums, *Heroes* and *Pride of the Nation*.

"We are both so delighted that you are able to join us in celebrating what we hope will be one of the happiest days of our lives."
The royal couple's introductory note to the official programme for the royal wedding

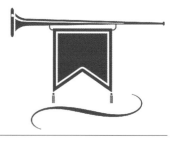

The Mall

TRADITIONALISTS KNOW there is only one place to be on any royal wedding day – The Mall. This imposing central boulevard, which runs from Buckingham Palace on its western end to Admiralty Arch on its eastern, has a unique red surface acting as VIP carpet leading to the Palace. It wasn't until the end of Queen Victoria's reign that a track through St. James's Park was reinvented as a grand ceremonial route, becoming the focus of national celebrations including the revels of VE Day.

On 29 April 2011 The Mall was an electrifying place to be, with crowds up to fourteen deep. Many had camped out the night before to get the best possible view. In places they even filled the Park's flowerbeds, or perched in trees like exotic birds. Above their heads fluttered The Mall's colourful parade of Union flags and, below those, a rippling Mexican wave of hand-held flags that carried the people's salute all the way down the route. Military brass bands entertained the throng and every passing vehicle, however innocuous, was met with cheers. When the cavalcade of cars heading towards Westminster Abbey finally came down The Mall, the applause was tumultuous, although everyone knew the main event was yet to come.

Once the service started it was broadcast down The Mall to a suddenly hushed multitude. Many retired to the grassy picnic land of St. James's Park, where there were also speakers relaying events. Here families set out rugs and students huddled over drinks in fancy-dress: stalls sold fish and chips, ice cream and champagne. Revellers sang along to the service's hymns and many stood for the National Anthem. Then everyone flooded back, refreshed, for the bridal procession, with many more joining from Whitehall to be close for the couple's balcony appearance.

If the crowd had been riotous before, now they were on fire. Strangers joshed with one another as if they were old friends; many had never attended a royal celebration previously and were bowled over by the heady atmosphere. Adults hoisted children to their shoulders and, at the back, people stood on stools and chairs to ensure a good view of the bride. Then they heard it: the far-off clatter of hooves like an advancing army. For all who had been waiting since the grey light of dawn, this was the climactic moment: Britain's future King returning with his bride. Everyone who stood on The Mall that day knew that they not only saw history in the making — they were part of it.

The Balcony

AT THE HEART OF ANY ROYAL WEDDING DAY is the couple's appearance on the balcony of Buckingham Palace, a tradition dating back to the time of Queen Victoria. This is the moment when procession and pageantry cease and the loyal multitude demands its more intimate reward: a kiss.

When Princess Diana offered her lips to Prince Charles in 1981, a precedent was established. The royal family is not given to public displays of affection, so the kiss was manna to romantics everywhere. Thirty years later, the throng was no less hungry for a royal embrace, flooding to fill the great space before the Palace gates, as they had done for other royal weddings, jubilees, and famously for VE day, when Winston Churchill joined the royal family on the balcony.

Every eye was trained on the balcony doors, looking for any teasing twitch of the curtain that might signal an appearance. The beaming new Duke and Duchess of Cambridge finally stepped out at 1.25pm and were greeted with a frenzy of cheers. When Catherine saw the vast crowd her eyes widened and she exclaimed "Oh wow!". The couple were alone on the balcony for a short while, before being joined by their bridesmaids, pageboys and immediate families. The crowd chanted "Kiss, kiss, kiss!", in a rising crescendo and a smiling William turned to Catherine and said: "Are you ready? Shall we kiss?" The cheering reached fever pitch as they leant towards one another, and their lips met briefly.

On the right hand side of the balcony Prince Harry turned and cracked a joke to the grimacing Duke of Edinburgh, making Pippa Middleton laugh too. On the other side, the Duchess of Cornwall and Prince Charles took turns to lift up Camilla's granddaughter, Eliza Lopes, so she could see the crowd. Minutes later Catherine and William obliged the masses again with a more lingering kiss.

Little Grace van Cutsem provided one of the day's most iconic images when she clamped her hands over her ears in reaction to the cheers. At 1.30 everyone lifted their eyes to the sky for the RAF fly-past. First came the Battle of Britain Memorial Flight, bringing lumps to the throat as a Lancaster, flanked by a Spitfire and a Hurricane, flew low over the Palace with the evocative drone of battles past. Then came two Typhoons and two Tornados flying in 'Windsor Formation', a tribute to current service. Shortly afterwards the wedding party returned to the reception.

The Main Players

The Abbey was a great stage and all eyes were trained on the *dramatis personae*: the beautiful bride and dashing groom, their families, attendants and the solemn men of God. Much hung upon the day's outcome. This, after all, was an evolution, the monarchy remodelling itself for the modern age. Yet the personal far outweighed the political. It was a day for parental pride, for a grandmother's delight, and for the joy of the newlyweds' siblings, who view bride and groom as their closest friends.

"Miss Middleton wished for her dress to combine tradition and modernity with the artistic vision that characterises Alexander McQueen."
A Clarence House spokesman

The Bride's Dress

NOT FOR THIRTY YEARS has a dress been so anticipated; but back in 1981 everyone knew the Emanuels had been chosen to design Diana's gown. This time the bride was determined to keep her designer's name under wraps, reserving her right to surprise the Prince and country and to outfox the press.

The moment when Catherine Middleton stepped out from the Goring Hotel, to admiring gasps, was her well-earned *coup de théâtre*. No one in the wider world had known until then that Sarah Burton of the label Alexander McQueen had landed the most prestigious job in fashion. Burton later admitted she had enjoyed "trying to hide", although she "blew it" when she dashed into the Goring Hotel on the eve of the wedding only slightly disguised with a fur hood.

The assignment was so secret that the lace-makers at the Royal School of Needlework at Hampton Court had been told their delicate creations were for a film costume. Suspicions must have been raised when the fabric's design involved the creation of lace roses, daffodils, shamrocks and thistles: the national emblems of England, Wales, Northern Ireland and Scotland. While toiling on the gown, the lace-makers washed their hands every thirty minutes to maintain the lustre of the soft ivory tulle. The intense craft, labour, sumptuous fabrics and symbolic emblems of Catherine's dress would have been familiar to any Tudor Queen, although everything here conspired to subtlety. This was not a gown that spoke of sovereignty, but one that whispered Catherine's homage to the British Isles.

Sarah Burton worked closely with Catherine to ensure the bride's own vision was exactly realised. The most obvious source of inspiration was the wedding dress of Grace Kelly, which also made seductive use of figure-skimming lace on the bodice over a full satin skirt. The bride's already slender waist was whittled by corsetry and padding to the hips – a trademark McQueen feature. Her ivory silk tulle veil floated like a gossamer cloud over her sculpted figure and put her face into radiant soft-focus.

The dress was made from ivory and white satin gazar sourced in Britain, and the floral theme was continued in its spreading skirt, designed to echo petals opening. The demure train was 8ft 10in long. The dress was breathtaking, without being overblown, regal, without being bombastic, and elegant, without stifling Catherine's freshness.

"I just want to do my best for her, and for Prince William, and that's all I want to do."
Shane Connolly, florist

Jewellery and Flowers

CATHERINE'S TASTE IS NATURALLY UNOSTENTATIOUS, so the loan of the Queen's delicate and understated 'halo' tiara was suited to her gamine beauty; the bride's 'something borrowed' was made by Cartier in 1936 and bought by the Duke of York (later George VI) for Elizabeth Bowes-Lyon. It was given to the Queen on her 18th birthday.

Catherine's acorn motif diamond earrings, commissioned by her parents from Robinson Pelham and inspired by the Middletons' new Coat of Arms, were 'something new'. Her wedding ring was a band of Welsh gold by Wartski.

The modest all-white bridal bouquet was made from seasonal flowers grown in Britain and further demonstrated Catherine's preference for elegant simplicity. The florist Shane Connolly, who also decorated the Abbey, worked with the bride to ensure each flower had its own poignant symbolism: lily of the valley signals the return of happiness, Sweet William stands for gallantry, ivy for fidelity, hyacinth for constancy and myrtle is the emblem of married love. The myrtle was gathered from a bush planted by Queen Victoria in 1845 at Osborne House and another plant grown from the Queen's own bridal myrtle.

"The Prince has an excellent physique so he really did justice to our tailoring skill."
Marlon Kashket, tailor to Prince William

"We worked together to get the look he wanted while using material to absorb the heat and make sure he didn't pass out in front of two billion people across the world."
Russell Kashket, tailor to Prince William

The Groom

PRINCE WILLIAM IS A MAN used to controlling his emotions and public persona. When Prince Harry made his best man's speech he said he realised William must be in love when his hitherto unsentimental brother started "cooing" down the phone to Catherine. On the Prince's wedding day the world got a glimpse of this emotional side. You could sense the groom's barely suppressed nerves when he arrived at Westminster Abbey at 10.18 with Prince Harry, who turned and asked "Are you ok?". An awestruck William replied, "Yes, it looks fantastic". He swiftly composed himself, and warmly greeted the Dean and Chapter of Westminster, family and friends in the Abbey as he awaited his bride.

Most commentators had expected Prince William to wear RAF uniform at his wedding, but instead he paid tribute to Northern Ireland and his most senior armed services' appointment: the honorary rank of Colonel of the Irish Guards. The Prince looked dashing in his mounted officer's uniform in guard of honour order, worn with a forage cap that bears the Guards' Insignia with its motto *Quis Separabit?* (Who shall separate us?). William's festive 'Guards' red' tunic made a striking background for his blue Garter sash and Garter star, RAF 'wings' and Golden Jubilee medal.

"'I am delighted that my brother has popped the question! It means I get a sister, which I have always wanted."
Prince Harry

Best Man and Maid of Honour

WITH TOUSLED HAIR, PUCKISH GRIN and the stiff walk of a man used to the saddle, Prince Harry looked every inch the cavalry officer as he accompanied his brother into the Abbey (although rumour had it that his slightly awkward gait was due to an ill-fated jump from a balcony at the Goring Hotel when leaving pre-wedding revels at 3am). The Prince looked exceptionally dashing in his Blues and Royals officer's uniform in Dismounted Review Order, with a forage cap carried in his hand. The Princes' tailor for the event, Marlon Kashket, explained how he had to sew a tiny Velcro compartment into the cuff of Prince Harry's uniform to keep the wedding ring safe, as ceremonial uniforms don't have pockets.

Traditionally royal grooms have 'supporters', so William's decision to make Harry his best man placed the traditions of an ordinary British family wedding at the heart of a state event and underlined the fact the brothers are genuinely best friends. The depth of affection between the pair was apparent as Harry bolstered William and steadied his nerves with jokes. When Catherine walked down the aisle it was Harry who turned his head to reassure William that his bride was on her way, telling his brother (according to a professional lip reader): "Well, she looks beautiful, I can tell you that."

Vivacious Pippa Middleton offered equally sterling support to her sister, gathering up Catherine's train when she stepped from the Rolls Royce and assuring her she looked "wonderful". Many onlookers were equally wonderstruck by Pippa's own slinky, ivory crepe gown (designed, like the bride's dress, by McQueen's Sarah Burton) with its revealing cowl neckline and teasing line of buttons down the back. By the day's end Twitter was heaving with tributes to the 'foxy' Pippa and five Facebook pages had been set up that were dedicated to her elegant figure. Just as many women wanted copycat versions of her frock as Catherine's.

Pippa performed her maid of honour duties with grace and aplomb, shepherding the two youngest bridesmaids through proceedings and always attending to her sister's needs, taking her bouquet or smoothing her train as needed. The Middleton sisters are every bit as close as the two Princes and the bride clearly wanted to showcase her younger sister's allure with a stunning dress.

When Pippa took Prince Harry's arm to follow the newly weds down the Abbey's nave the watching world delighted in seeing the two high-spirited younger siblings briefly united.

Top left: Prince Harry's Forage Cap carried the badge of the Blues and Royals, which features the insignia of the Most Noble Order of the Garter with the Queen's cipher. The Prince wore aiguillettes, a cross-belt and gold waist belt with sword slings, but no sword. He also wore Wings of the Army Air Corps and Golden Jubilee and Afghanistan Campaign medals.

Above: Harry and Pippa walk arm-in-arm down the aisle at the end of the service.

Above: Catherine Middleton's 27-year-old sister also wore a dress designed by Sarah Burton of Alexander McQueen. Her dress was made of ivory satin crepe, with the same embroidery and organza-covered buttons as her sister's wedding dress. Miss Middleton wore her hair half-up, half-down, clipped with lily of the valley flowers at the back.

Her parents had given her a pair of floral diamond earrings designed by Robinson Pelham.

"They were going to wear swords but then we thought they might have a swordfight in the Abbey..."
Russell Kashket, royal tailor, on the pageboys' outfits

Bridesmaids and Pageboys

As with any wedding, the young bridesmaids and pageboys captivated everyone; one guest in the Abbey described how a clutch of usually implacable diplomats collapsed into coos at the sight of the wide-eyed children. Although Catherine chose her sister, Pippa, as maid of honour, the younger attendants were all drawn from Prince William's closest family ties and friendships – a sign of how close Catherine has become to William's circle in their eight years together.

The Queen was reportedly thrilled by the inclusion of her seven-year-old granddaughter, Lady Louise Windsor (daughter of the Earl of Wessex) as a bridesmaid. The Queen's eight-year-old great-niece, the Hon Margarita Armstrong-Jones (Viscount Linley's daughter) was also picked. And William paid tribute to his stepmother Camilla by choosing her bewitching little granddaughter Eliza Lopes as an attendant, although it was his goddaughter Grace van Cutsem who threatened to steal the show with her huge blue eyes and ferociously unimpressed demeanour.

Pippa Middleton ushered the two three-year-olds throughout proceedings and Prince Harry was later revealed to have entertained them with a cheap wiggly-worm toy.

The two impish pageboys performed their roles immaculately, while never appearing oppressed by the day's solemnity. Ten-year-old William Lowther-Pinkerton is the son of Prince William's Private Secretary Jamie Lowther-Pinkerton. The Prince's godson, eight-year-old Tom Pettifer, is the son of Tiggy Pettifer (formerly Legge-Bourke), who acted as an amalgam of nanny and surrogate big sister for William and Harry following their parents' divorce. The boys wore scarlet tunics, ivory breeches and crimson and gold sashes inspired by uniforms worn by Foot Guards' officers in the 1820s.

The delightful ballerina-length bridesmaids' dresses were made by children's-wear designer Nicki Macfarlane and her daughter Charlotte. They were cut from the same ivory and white satin gazar as the bride's gown, with box-pleated skirts and puff sleeves, and then hand-finished with delicate English cluny lace. The sashes were made of pale gold wild silk, tied at the back in a generous bow and the girls' names and the wedding date were hand-embroidered onto the lining of every dress, as a memento of the day. Their flowers were arranged by Catherine's florist, Shane Connolly, who said the ivy and lily of the valley headdresses were modelled on those worn at Carole Middleton's wedding in 1980.

Top left: The two older
bridesmaids, Lady Louise
Windsor and the Hon Margarita
Armstrong-Jones, looking
enchanting in their ballerina-
length ivory gowns, share
their excitement with the two
pageboys, William Lowther-
Pinkerton and Tom Pettifer,
who were styled as Regency
Foot Guards' officers. The
children had attended rehearsals
together and clearly enjoyed
one another's company.

Above: Pippa Middleton
ushers the younger attendants
into Westminster Abbey,
holding the hands of the two
three-year-olds, Grace van
Cutsem and Eliza Lopes. The
sumptuous gold bows on
the bridesmaids' dresses are
displayed to good effect, as are
the pageboys' gold epaulettes
and the magnificent gold tassels
on their ceremonial sashes.
Lady Louise Windsor turns
to smile shyly at the crowd.

"I love seeing the faces of the public when they meet the Queen, and when she gives them that special smile. It makes me feel so proud of her."
Angela Kelly, royal desgner

Right: Prince Charles arrives at Westminster Abbey with the Duchess of Cornwall. The Prince holds the rank of Admiral and was wearing his blue Royal Navy Number One Dress (ceremonial) with a blue Order of the Garter sash. Camilla wore an Anna Valentine coat and dress.

The Royal Family

THE QUEEN IN HER PRIMROSE YELLOW Angela Kelly ensemble, with its joyful burst of beaded sunrays round the neckline, radiated quiet pleasure. The symbolism of her wearing Queen Mary's 'True Lover's Knot' brooch was clear. The monarch is not given to public displays of affection, but on her grandson's wedding day her approval was evident. "Excellent" she said at one juncture, and "Amazing" at another.

Prince Philip, on the eve of his 90th birthday, looked alternately pleased and wry in his Grenadier Guards uniform. Prince Charles displayed paternal pride throughout the day, while the Duchess of Cornwall looked moved to tears at times. Prince Andrew escorted his daughters Princesses Beatrice and Eugenie, who sported two of Philip Treacy's more outré hat designs, while the Earl and Countess of Wessex gazed proudly at their bridesmaid daughter Lady Louise Windsor. Princess Anne is her father's equal for wry looks, but she could be forgiven for her focus being on the year's other celebrated bride, her daughter Zara Phillips. Also seated prominently in the Abbey's South Lantern were the Duke and Duchess of Kent, Prince and Princess Michael of Kent, Princess Alexandra and the Duke and Duchess of Gloucester and their families.

"Really nice and down to earth."
Sarah Burton, the designer of Catherine's
wedding dress, on the Middleton family

The Middleton Family

THROUGHOUT PRINCE WILLIAM'S courtship of Catherine
Middleton her family has been subject to media scrutiny and
speculation. Yet the Middletons have always behaved with
dignity and discretion, never commenting on their royal
connection. This has won them widespread respect, as has
the enviable closeness of the family.

On the wedding day, however, it was the family's elegance and
good looks that caught the eye, as well as their obvious pride
in Catherine. Michael Middleton's emotion as he escorted
his daughter down the aisle of Westminster Abbey, tightly
clutching her hand, and lifted her veil at the High Altar was
tangible. Carole Middleton was equally emotional, barely able
to sing during the service's three hymns and clearly battling
back tears at times.

All fathers feel some sadness in handing their daughters to
another's care, but in Catherine Middleton's case a real
transition occurred: those who marry into the royal family
are duty bound to serve and live their lives in the public
glare. Catherine's parents clearly felt the solemnity of the
moment, as well as its joy. The bride's siblings James and
Pippa radiated less complicated pleasure at her happiness.

Left: The maid of honour Pippa Middleton in her Sarah Burton-designed gown. She was so widely admired that one newspaper asked of the professional party organiser, "Is this the most eligible woman in Britain?".

Above: Michael and Carole Middleton leave Westminster Abbey. Carole was the epitome of elegance in a chic sky blue wool crepe coatdress over a silk shantung 'Sydney' day dress, by Catherine Walker. Her hat was by Berkshire-based Jane Corbett and her pendant from jeweller Robinson Pelham, who made individual pieces for each family member. The Middletons were keen to fly the flag for British fashion and craftsmanship.

Above: James Middleton looks dapper in a morning coat, as he waits to escort his mother into the Abbey. The Middletons are known for their close family ties. James shares a Kensington flat with his sister Pippa and the duo are Catherine's closest confidantes. All of the three children have helped out at times with their parents' party accessories business.

Carole's composure on the wedding day was the perfect riposte to the mean-spirited comments she had endured from some quarters of the press during William's courtship of Catherine about her ambitions for her daughter. Every loving mother believes her daughter is good enough for a Prince, and the woman who grew a tabletop business into a thriving mail order firm will never be one to set limits for her children.

Queen Margrethe of Denmark is followed by King Harald and Queen Sonja of Norway and Grand Duchess Maria Teresa of Luxembourg with Grand Duke Henri, and Belgium's Crown Princess Mathilde with Crown Prince Philippe. Finally Crown Princess Máxima of the Netherlands with Crown Prince Willem-Alexander.

VIP Guests

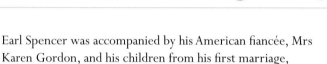

THE TERM 'A FAMILY WEDDING' takes on different connotations when the groom is a Prince of the realm and many kin are foreign royalty. Around forty of the guests were overseas' royalty, greeting and gossiping amongst themselves like any relatives at a marriage ceremony, before taking their seats in the Abbey's South Lantern. The group included Queen Sofia of Spain, her son Crown Prince Felipe and his wife, the former TV anchorwoman Princess Letizia. King Constantine and Queen Anne-Marie of Greece were present, with their son Crown Prince Pavlos and his American heiress wife, Crown Princess Marie-Chantal, while Prince Albert of Monaco escorted his fiancée Charlene Wittstock. Crown Princess Victoria of Sweden held the hand of new husband and former personal trainer Prince Daniel.

The Yang di-Pertuan Agong of Malaysia was there and leading members of Arab royal families. Diplomats were relieved, however, when the Crown Prince of Bahrain sent his apologies, owing to political unrest in his country, following the 'Arab Spring' uprisings and accusations of state brutality.

Across from the foreign royalty in the North Lantern sat close members of the late Diana Princess of Wales's family.

Earl Spencer was accompanied by his American fiancée, Mrs Karen Gordon, and his children from his first marriage, Lady Kitty, Lady Eliza and Lady Amelia.

Also in prominent seats were members of the Diplomatic Corps, Commonwealth Prime Ministers, the chiefs of Britain's armed forces and Britain's religious leaders, including The Chief Rabbi Lord Sacks, Imam Mohammad Raza and Cardinal Cormac Murphy-O'Connor. Cardinal Sean Brady, Primate of All Ireland, attended, in an unprecedented move for the Catholic head of the Irish Church. Lord-Lieutenants for the UK were also included.

Because Prince William is second in line to the throne the wedding was not deemed to be a full state occasion, so foreign heads of state, such as President Obama, and former British Prime Ministers, such as Tony Blair and Gordon Brown, were not invited. The former Conservative leader Sir John Major was asked, as he was made guardian to Princes William and Harry following Diana's death. Current British politicians who were present included the Prime Minister David Cameron, the Leader of the Opposition Ed Miliband and the Mayor of London Boris Johnson.

"Everyone has been joking about it and offering to go in my place, but that's one seat I won't be giving up."
John Hayley, landlord of the Old Boot Inn in Bucklebury, on receiving his invitation

Victoria and David Beckham excited the crowds with their attendance, but the celebrity quotient was refreshingly small. In the Abbey they rubbed shoulders with guests from all walks of life who had crossed paths with the royal couple.

Other Guests

THE SCENE INSIDE WESTMINSTER ABBEY resembled a grand country wedding on an epic scale, with a sea of flamboyant hats, jewel-coloured costumes and exuberant greetings. A thousand of the 1,900 guests were friends of the bride and groom and no area of their lives had been overlooked.

A clutch of the Middleton clan were seated close to the High Altar in the Abbey's North Lantern, including Catherine's flamboyant uncle Gary in an immaculate morning coat. Prominent space was also allotted to the couple's closest friends, such as William's pals Thomas van Straubenzee and Hugh van Cutsem (father of bridesmaid Grace), as well as the St. Andrews crowd, such as the couple's student housemates Fergus Boyd and Olivia Bleasdale. Catherine asked her jockey friend Sam Waley-Cohen, Marlborough school friend Alicia Fox-Pitt, her former employers Belle and John Robinson from fashion chain Jigsaw, and her photography mentor Alistair Morrison.

The royal couple showed no insecurities about inviting former loves. Catherine asked ex-beau Rupert Finch, while William asked Jecca Craig, Olivia Hunt and Arabella Musgrave, who were once romantically linked to him.

It was touching to see how William remembered those who had helped him from his earliest days. His childhood nanny Barbara Barnes was present and Tiggy Pettifer (formerly Legge-Bourke) who looked after William and Harry for Prince Charles following his divorce. He also asked his old housemaster from Eton, Dr Andrew Gailey, his armed forces comrades, and his long time hairdresser, Mandy Turner.

Over 80 top executives from the charities for which the Prince acts as patron were invited. Catherine showed her attachment to Bucklebury, the Berkshire village where she grew up, by asking John Hayley, the landlord of the village pub, and Hash and Chan Shingadia, who run the local store.

The celebrity quotient was refreshingly small; the stars who attended were friends, or had helped with the Prince's charities. They included Victoria and David Beckham and Sir Elton John and his partner David Furnish. The comedian Rowan Atkinson attended, alongside singer Joss Stone, film director Guy Ritchie, photographer Mario Testino and the broadcasters Dan Snow, Ben Fogle and Tom Bradby. The sporting world was represented by Sir Trevor Brooking, Ian Thorpe, Sir Clive Woodward and Gareth Thomas.

The Party Begins

After the solemnity of the marriage service came the joy of a nationwide party. Hundreds toasted the bride and groom at Buckingham Palace, but millions raised their glasses across Great Britain and the globe. Onlookers recognised themselves in Catherine and William: the couple who met at university, who courted and lived together, split and then made up. When William drove his bride away in his father's vintage Aston Martin, it was more fairytale than any glass carriage.

"From where I was, and from their point of view, it was two families coming together and that was the feeling – the sense of family and love going between everyone."

Hugo Burnard, Royal Wedding photographer

Official Photographs

SOCIETY PHOTOGRAPHER HUGO BURNARD was chosen to take the official wedding pictures, which were staged in Buckingham Palace's magnificent Throne Room. Burnard (who also took the photos for Princes Charles's wedding to Camilla Parker Bowles) cycled to the Palace with his team of helpers, who had staged dress rehearsals before the event with stand-ins and stopwatches. The photographer calculated that he had just 44 minutes to shoot the photographs. In the event, he managed to complete the shoot in a lightning-quick 26 minutes, using sweets to bribe the youngest children into keeping still.

The resulting images achieve the rare feat of being suitably majestic, yet utterly relaxed. The joy of the day radiates from the two families' wide smiles. The photos knowingly echo those from Prince Charles's marriage to Diana, but this time round the groom is beaming and shows no reserve, while the tight bond with his bride is unmistakable. In the picture taken with her attendants Catherine's hand rests naturally on William's knee. These are the iconic images no one would have believed possible a generation ago: the second heir to the throne marrying a young woman who is neither royal, nor an aristocrat.

Left: Two families united. This is a formal photo taken in Buckingham Palace's Throne Room, but the expressions are joyful – although the three-year-old Grace van Cutsem is still unimpressed. The eagle-eyed can see little Eliza Lopes is still clutching the tiny pink wiggly worm toy given to her by Prince Harry to keep her engaged during the day.

Left: A relaxed Duke and Duchess of Cambridge surrounded by their attendants. Pageboy William Lowther-Pinkerton strikes a military pose, while mischievous Tom Pettifer tilts behind Catherine's head. The picture echoes the wedding photo of Prince Charles sitting with Princess Diana, who had collapsed in a merry heap with her attendants. Bridesmaid Margarita Armstrong-Jones is even sitting in the same place that her aunt, the then Lady Sarah Armstrong Jones, occupied for Diana's photograph.

"We are so lucky to have her."
Prince Charles in a short address to guests
at the afternoon reception

The Daytime Reception

THE QUEEN HOSTED A RECEPTION for 650 people at Buckingham
Palace, where guests were served canapés made from the best of
British ingredients. This was the larger and far more formal of
the day's two parties, tailored to the sensibilities of the monarch
and dignitaries. Claire Jones, the official harpist to the Prince of
Wales, provided musical entertainment.

Invitees included family, friends and foreign royalty, as
well as representatives from the couple's official lives.
During the course of the reception Governors-General and
Commonwealth Prime Ministers were presented to the
Queen and to the bride and groom. The wedding cakes were
cut during the afternoon and Prince Charles made a short
speech, saying Catherine was the daughter he had never had.

Showing perspicacity and tact, the Queen and Duke of
Edinburgh vacated the Palace for the weekend after the
afternoon's celebrations, enabling their grandson and his
bride to have a more unbuttoned evening party. William
and Catherine also left the Palace briefly, in Prince Charles's
ribbon-festooned 1969 Aston Martin DB6 Mk 2 Volante,
which had been given the temporary number plate 'JU5T
WED', for Clarence House and a couple of hours' privacy.

RECEPTION

Canapés

Guests were served a selection of canapés, including:

Cornish Crab Salad on Lemon Blini
Pressed Duck Terrine with Fruit Chutney
Roulade of Goats Cheese with Caramelised Walnuts
Assortment of Palmiers and Cheese Straws
Scottish Smoked Salmon Rose on Beetroot Blini
Miniature Watercress and Asparagus Tart
Poached Asparagus Spears with Hollandaise Sauce for Dipping
Quails Eggs with Celery Salt
Scottish Langoustines with Lemon Mayonnaise
Pressed Confit of Pork Belly with Crayfish and Crackling
Wild Mushroom and Celeriac Chausson
Bubble and Squeak with Confit Shoulder of Lamb
Grain Mustard and Honey-glazed Chipolatas
Smoked Haddock Fishcake with Pea Guacamole
Miniature Yorkshire Pudding with Roast Fillet of Beef and
Horseradish Mousse

Gâteau Opera
Blood Orange Pâté de Fruit
Raspberry Financier
Rhubarb Crème Brulée Tartlet
Passion Fruit Praline
White Chocolate Ganache Truffle
Milk Chocolate Praline with Nuts
Dark Chocolate Ganache Truffle

Guests were served Pol Roger NV Brut Réserve Champagne
with a selection of other soft and alcoholic drinks.

Ingredients

All the ingredients for the canapés were carefully
sourced from Royal Warrant holding companies using
UK-based ingredients.

Left: The White Drawing Room at Buckingham Palace with its spectacular John Nash ceiling and pilasters incorporating Garter Stars, was one of the 19 opulent state rooms used for the afternoon reception, which also included the Music Room, Picture Gallery and State Dining Room. Priceless masterpieces from the Royal Collection were on display, including works by Canaletto, Rembrandt and Rubens.

Above: The new Duchess of Cambridge talks to the Welsh-born Prime Minister of Australia Julia Gillard and her partner Tim Mathieson at the wedding reception. The afternoon event involved the formal introductions, with line-ups of dignitaries, that will fast become a staple part of the bride's future life. Catherine displays the sort of ease and charm with strangers that made Princess Diana so popular.

"Catherine did not want it to be seven feet tall, she didn't want it to be towering and thin, and I think we succeeded."
Fiona Cairns, pastry chef

The Wedding Cake

THE DAY'S THEME OF GLORIOUS TRADITION, tempered by youthful modernity, was followed right through to the cakes. A Palladian pile of a wedding cake was ordered from Leicestershire pastry chef Fiona Cairns, while McVitie's created a chocolate biscuit cake at Prince William's request.

Cairns and her team spent five weeks labouring on their formal eight-tiered confection, which was made from 17 individual fruit cakes. Catherine requested that the cake incorporate elements from the Joseph Lambeth technique of cake decoration, where intricate piping is used to make three-dimensional motifs, such as scrolls, leaves and flowers. The final decorative touches were added in Buckingham Palace's imposing Picture Gallery (*top*). Cairns cleverly incorporated some of the room's architectural details, "so the garlands on the walls were reproduced loosely on the fourth tier – we've used roses, acorns ivy leaves, apple blossom and bridal rose."

William's biscuit cake was created from a favourite royal family recipe and was somewhat simpler in construction: three cocoa-laden slabs. But McVitie's added their own flourish in the shape of white chocolate water lilies fit for a Prince. Both cakes were cut at the afternoon reception.

THE CAKE

Each of the 17 different flower designs on the official wedding cake has their own individual meaning according to the Language of Flowers. They include:

White Rose - National emblem of England
Daffodil - National emblem of Wales, new beginnings
Shamrock - National emblem of Ireland
Thistle - National emblem of Scotland
Acorns, Oak Leaf - Strength, endurance
Myrtle - Love
Ivy - Wedded Love, marriage
Lily of the Valley - Sweetness, humility
Rose (Bridal) - Happiness, love
Sweet William - 'Grant me one smile'
Honeysuckle - 'The Bond of Love'
Apple Blossom - Preference, good fortune
White Heather - Protection, wishes will come true
Jasmine (White) - Amiability
Daisy - Innocence, beauty, simplicity
Orange Blossom - Marriage, eternal love, fruitfulness
Lavender - Ardent attachment, devotion, success and luck

"William didn't have a romantic bone in his body before he met Kate."
Prince Harry's best man's speech

The Evening Reception

ONLY 300 GUESTS received the day's most exclusive invitation – to the sit-down dinner at Buckingham Palace. Most were from the closest circle of the bride and groom, although Prince Charles and Camilla and Michael and Carole Middleton also asked friends. The newlyweds made their entrance shortly after seven; they joined their guests for drinks before leading the way into the ballroom, which had been filled with round tables. Each was set for ten guests and bore the name of a place dear to the couple, such as 'St. Andrews', in honour of their university days. Chef Anton Mosimann created his menu from the finest British ingredients, including lamb from Highgrove.

For many, the highlight of proceedings was Prince Harry's best man's speech, which he delivered wearing a fez. Guests roared with laughter when he dubbed his brother "The Dude" and mocked William's receding hairline, saying he was sorry Catherine had to marry "a bald man". He also told, in true younger brother style, how William had fought with him when they were small and nearly shot him with an air rifle. The bride had to wipe a tear away when her new brother-in-law said he loved her as "a sister" and that he was inspired by the couple's relationship.

Michael Middleton's speech was also praised; he told guests that he knew matters were "getting serious" when William landed a helicopter in his back garden and nearly blew his roof off. Then it was the groom's turn to address his guests; he paid tribute to his late mother, Princess Diana and praised his "beautiful" bride "Mrs Wales". Finally two of William's old school friends, Thomas van Straubenzee and James Meade, performed a double act, teasing the prince.

Then Prince Harry, as master of ceremonies, led the way into the Palace's Throne Room, which had been transformed into a nightclub, complete with cocktail bar, sofas and a dance floor with strobe lights. The singer Ellie Goulding performed an energetic two-hour set, starting with the bride and groom dancing to her version of Elton John's 'Your Song'. Then a disco took over, mixing 60s' classics with contemporary artists and sending booming bass lines down The Mall. At 2.30am the party survivors took to the dance floor for the final track, singing along with bride and groom to the Beatles' 'She Loves You'. The celebrations finished with fireworks, on the Palace lawn, and the departure of bride and groom to a suite at the Palace. It was an an unprecedented event in Palace annals, described as "the party of the decade."

Above: The Duchess of Cambridge leaves Clarence House for the evening reception with The Duchess of Cornwall. The bride had changed into a strapless white satin gazar gown with diamenté embroidered waist detail, teamed with a white angora bolero cardigan designed by Sarah Burton of Alexander McQueen. The bride is close to Camilla, who has given her astute advice on joining the royal family.

Above: The Duke of Cambridge and the Prince of Wales lead the way from Clarence House to the waiting cars. Father and son looked dashing in black tie, finally able to relax after months of preparation. They discussed how three-year-old bridesmaid Grace van Cutsem had clamped her hands over her ears on the Palace balcony. William said sympathetically, "Did you see how terrified Grace looked?"

Union flags fluttered the length and breadth of the British Isles as 29th April was declared a national holiday. Red, white and blue was the dress code of the day. Fancy dress was *de rigueur*; the streets were thronged with parody princesses, extravagant hats, William and Catherine face masks, and a riot of inventive interpretations of the patriotic theme of the day.

The Prime Minister David Cameron said: "My message to everyone who wants to have a street party is: I'm having one and I want you to go ahead and have one too. The truth is that this is a great chance for communities to come together and celebrate. So go on – bring out the bunting and let's make this a day to remember. For everyone."

Street Parties

ROYAL WEDDING FERVOUR took a while to build in Britain: the public lacked recent practice in displays of nationwide patriotism. Two weeks before the big day the Prime Minister David Cameron urged Britons to follow his example and hold a street party – and thousands were spurred into action. By 29th April there were over 5,500 applications across the nation to close roads and hold parties and a great wave of royalist sentiment had finally gripped the nation.

London topped the party list with 800 street celebrations, as well as huge gatherings, with giant TV screens, in Hyde Park and Trafalgar Square. There was barely a corner of Britain that didn't have some form of festivity. Cardiff hosted 50 street parties, in Weston-super-Mare the bash was on the Pier. The High Street in Alcester, Warwickshire, was entirely closed off for one of Britain's largest shindigs. In Manchester people partied in the city centre, while in Putney the Ahmadiyva Muslim Community organised a party for residents living close to the London Mosque.

Scotland's revels naturally centred on St. Andrews University, where William and Catherine met. The event, which attracted thousands, kicked off in St. Salvator's Quadrangle

with a champagne breakfast. In Anglesey, where William is based as an RAF search and rescue helicopter pilot, the Agricultural Showground staged a 'One Big Day' event with a fly-past by William's colleagues. Another hub of wild celebration was Catherine's home village of Bucklebury in Berkshire, where they staged duck-racing, discos and a three-hour long commemorative bell ringing session.

Britain's smallest street party was thrown in Bradford by 63-year-old Judith Watkinson, who put a table on the pavement outside her bungalow. She said: "I've got my royal teapot, cups and saucers and I am flying the flag for all the little people who love the royals." The Prime Minister hosted 90 pensioners and schoolchildren at Downing Street; his wife Samantha made celebratory cupcakes and Larry, the No. 10 cat, wore a Union flag bowtie for the occasion.

All over Britain flags fluttered from windows, little girls were dressed as princesses and boys had their faces painted red, white and blue. Adults sported Union flag bowler hats, young women wore wedding gowns and sashes saying "It should have been me!" At last the slow swell of patriotic feeling had turned into wedding fever.

A global phenomenon: (clockwise from top left): Troops in Afghanistan, the centre of Berlin, Times Square in New York, a beach in Dubai, the British embassy in Kathmandu and Penzance Primary School, Durban. The BBC alone, through its global arm, beamed live coverage to Asia, Europe, Africa, Australia and America. British servicemen and women watched in Afghanistan and Iraq, and Britons abroad turned British language schools and churches into improvised cinemas. New York's Times Square hosted a huge royal wedding celebration and outdoor screenings were also staged at holiday beaches and even shopping malls in cities as diverse as Berlin and Nairobi.

TV Coverage

IN 1981 THE TELEVISION AUDIENCE for the wedding of Prince Charles to Lady Diana Spencer totalled 750 million. Thirty years later the total broadcast audience for the marriage of the couple's son was estimated at over two billion – once those who watched the coverage on the internet had been included. An estimated 8,000 broadcast journalists and technical staff from around the world descended on London and temporary studios were erected just outside Buckingham Palace and opposite Westminster Abbey.

American audiences were more eager in their anticipation of the wedding than the British, loving the Cinderella story of Catherine Middleton's rise from middle-class girl to royal duchess. Twenty three million viewers from the US tuned in before dawn on eleven networks to watch live coverage of the wedding.

The CNN presenter Richard Quest, who was one of the channel's anchors for the wedding coverage, said: "The Americans see it as a reality show, a soap opera, which perhaps people in Britain miss because this is about their future head of state and his consort." Some American commentators were baffled by the proliferation of hats,

which aren't a set feature of Stateside weddings. Shep Smith of Fox News said of one woman's fascinator: "Look at this dang thing. What in the heck is that thing on her noggin?" In China, Phoenix TV screened the ceremony to a million viewers. One housewife, Yang Xiaohe, spoke for many when she said: "What really draws me is the tradition and ceremony, there isn't anything akin to royalty in China and there's just something so magical about it."

In Britain, 26.2 million viewers tuned in to live coverage across the television networks. At the BBC a sober Huw Edwards and Sophie Raworth were anchors, while ITV paired bouncy Phillip Schofield with Julie Etchingham. When the royal wedding party returned to the Palace, offering a pause in proceedings, there was a huge surge in electrical demand as television cameras switched back to the TV studios. The 2,400 MW boost at 12.40pm was equivalent to nearly a million kettles being boiled at once.

Some broadcast experts believe one in three of the world's population viewed the royal wedding in some form: an extraordinary statistic that gives the lie to those who claim the modern monarchy is an irrelevance.

A Royal Life

The grandeur and glamour of palace life – seen here at a Victorian ball in Buckingham Palace – is inevitably associated with royalty. But the Royal Households, with their enormous retinues of aides, private secretaries, spokesmen, ladies-in-waiting and equerries, are first and foremost a complex mechanism that manages the public face of royalty – from walkabouts and state visits to patronage of charities. In this era, modern royalty must be media savvy as well as majestic.

The Duke and Duchess of Cambridge will have access to a rich range of historic London palaces and magnificent rural retreats, the enviable birthright of a royal prince. For the time being, they are making Kensington Palace their official London residence.

Royal Palaces

CLARENCE HOUSE

Clarence House is the official residence of the Prince of Wales, his wife the Duchess of Cornwall, and his son Prince Harry. It stands on The Mall and is adjoined by Engine Court to St. James's Palace, whose gardens it shares. The house was commissioned by William, Duke of Clarence (later King William IV) and built between 1825–27 to a design by John Nash. It was remodelled, enlarged and restored after bomb damage in World War II, but three storeys of Nash's original building remain, along with several early 19th-century chimney-pieces and ceilings.

Clarence House was occupied by – amongst others – two of Queen Victoria's sons, Prince

Alfred and Prince Arthur, and by Princess Elizabeth and the Duke of Edinburgh. Clarence House became identified in the public's imagination with Queen Elizabeth the Queen Mother, who lived there as her official residence from 1953 until her death in 2002. It is open to the public from August to October each year.

ST. JAMES'S PALACE

St. James's Palace was built between 1532 and 1540 by King Henry VIII. It remains the senior palace of the Sovereign, and the Court to which foreign ambassadors and high commissioners are accredited. The State Apartments are used for entertaining during in-coming State visits, as well

as for other ceremonial and formal occasions. The Accession Council meets there following the death of a monarch, and the accession of the new monarch is announced from the Proclamation Gallery overlooking Engine Court.

Much still remains of the original red-brick quadrangular Tudor manor, including two Tudor rooms in the State Apartments and the Chapel Royal where King Charles I received Holy Communion before his execution. William IV was the last Sovereign to use the Palace as a residence, and it increasingly came to be used only for formal occasions, such as balls, and for presentation at court. It is Princess Anne's official London residence.

BUCKINGHAM PALACE

Built in 1703 for John Sheffield, 1st Duke of Buckingham, King George III acquired Buckingham House (as it was then known) in 1761 as a residence for his wife Queen Charlotte. Fourteen of the King and Queen's fifteen children were born there.

King George III employed architects Sir William Chambers and James Wyatt to make alterations and improvements, including the striking octagon library (*above*), and the next monarch, King George IV, asked his favourite architect, John Nash, to convert the house into a palace. Nash enlarged and remodelled the existing house, forming three wings around a central courtyard, and created a series of remarkably ornate State and Semi-State rooms.

In the centre of the principal floor is the Music Room where many royal christenings have been performed, and where the Queen receives guests during State Visits.

The next monarch, King William IV, preferred to stay in comfort at Clarence House, but in 1837, on her accession to the throne, Queen Victoria chose to use Buckingham Palace as her official residence. It was during Victoria's reign that the east front, joining the north and south wings and closing in the quadrangle, was created to make its present form. The new front looks out onto The Mall and St. James's Park, and contains the balcony where the royal family appears to greet the public at times of national rejoicing and in times of crisis.

KENSINGTON PALACE

A firm favourite of members of the royal family, Queen Victoria was especially fond of her childhood home and saved it from demolition during the second half of the 19th century.

This Jacobean mansion, originally named Nottingham House, became a royal residence when King William III bought it from the Earl of Nottingham, in 1689 for about £18,000. The king engaged Christopher Wren to extend and improve the house, and Nicholas Hawksmoor was appointed his clerk of works. Wren's embellishments included the addition of 'pavilions' to each corner of the house, and royal apartments were built in the south-east and north-west. A private road led from the palace to Hyde Park Corner.

Kensington House, as it was re-named upon completion in August 1690, was seen as a rural retreat, and it was not until later generations of royal occupants had created grander embellishments that it became known as Kensington Palace.

Queen Victoria installed various members of her family in the apartments; the future Queen Mary was born there in 1867. Parliament funded restorations on the understanding that the State Apartments would be opened to the public, which duly occurred on 24 May 1899, Victoria's 80th birthday.

Once the home of the Prince and Princess of Wales, it remained Princess Diana's official residence until her death in 1997. It is currently the home of the Duke and Duchess of Gloucester, the Duke and Duchess of Kent, Prince and Princess Michael of Kent and the Duke and Duchess of Cambridge.

Royal Retreats

WINDSOR CASTLE

This is the only royal residence that has been in continuous use since its foundation by William the Conqueror in the 1070s. The Queen uses the castle both as a private home, where she often spends weekends, and as a royal residence where she receives and entertains foreign Heads of State. The Queen takes up official residence in the castle for a month over Easter, and for a week in June when she attends the Garter Service and Royal Ascot. Christmas is also usually spent at Windsor.

Windsor Castle covers an area of some 13 acres. It has over a thousand rooms, which include royal and guest apartments, sixteen State Apartments, and accommodation for the 500

or more people who live and work in the castle, making it the largest inhabited castle in the world. Much of the castle's present day appearance, both inside and out, is due to alterations and additions instigated by King George IV and his architect, Sir Jeffry Wyatville who, in the 1820s and at colossal expense, refaced and heightened many of the buildings, adding towers, turrets and crenellations to give the castle a Gothic look.

The Queen gives state banquets in St. George's Hall (185 feet long and 30 feet wide), the largest room in the castle. This is also where the Knights of the Garter assemble in full robes before processing to their service in St. George's Chapel. The Hall is splendidly

decorated with the coats of arms of every Knight of the Garter created since the Order was constituted by Edward III in 1348, in a tradition which continues to this day.

Another monarch closely associated with Windsor Castle is King Charles II, who made extensive alterations to the State Apartments in the 1670s, employing Antonio Verrio for murals and ceiling paintings, and Grinling Gibbons for wood-carving. They produced a set of extravagant, baroque interiors. King Charles also laid out the Long Walk leading from the castle into Windsor Great Park.

The State Apartments contain some of the best works of art in the Royal Collection, including paintings by Holbein,

Van Dyck, Rembrandt, Rubens, Durer, Honthorst, Canaletto, Gainsborough, Zoffany, Stubbs and Clouet.

The quadrangle in the Upper Ward is the setting for numerous colourful ceremonies, particularly the arrival of foreign Heads of State, who enter the castle in horse-drawn carriages through the George IV Gateway. It was the Upper Ward that suffered most in a major fire that occurred during renovations at Windsor Castle on 20 November 1992. The blaze caused severe damage to nine principal state rooms, and the restoration work was paid for by opening Buckingham Palace to the public at selected times of the year, and by introducing charges for public access to Windsor Great Park.

SANDRINGHAM HOUSE

In 1862 Queen Victoria bought this private residence, set in some 20,000 acres, for her son and heir, the Prince of Wales (later King Edward VII), and his new bride, Alexandra of Denmark. Only two years after moving in the Prince found the house was too small to accommodate his growing family and to entertain his friends, so he commissioned A. J. Humbert to raze the house and replace it with a new building.

The resulting red-brick neo-Jacobean building with stone dressings and gabled roofs, completed in 1870, is an odd but attractive mixture of styles. Later additions were a ballroom in 1881 and a conservatory in 1887. Fourteen rooms on the upper storeys were destroyed in a fire during the preparations for the Prince of Wales's 50th birthday in 1891.

The grounds of Sandringham House have been greatly enjoyed by generations of royal youngsters. Such was King Edward VII's fondness for shooting on the estate he ordered all the clocks to be set half-an-hour ahead of Greenwich Mean Time to allow more time for the sport. This tradition of 'Sandringham Time' was kept on the estate from 1901 until 1936 when King Edward VIII swept the custom away.

Queen Alexandra, her two sons Prince Albert Victor, Duke of Clarence, and King George V, and his son King George VI all died at Sandringham. The Queen has traditionally spent the anniversary of her father's death on 6 February 1952, and her own accession, with her family at Sandringham House, which is the private property of the royal family and not a part of the Crown Estate.

BALMORAL

Balmoral Castle is a large country house situated by the River Dee, in the parish of Crathie, Aberdeenshire. It was bought by Queen Victoria and the Prince Consort in 1852, and it remains the private property of the Sovereign. The castle commands views of a rich and varied landscape. It has a working estate of 49,000 acres including farmland, forestry, grouse moors and managed deer herds.

Victoria and Albert sought Balmoral for its healthy climate, and their first visit was made in 1848. The neighbouring estate of Birkhall, where the Prince of Wales and Duchess of Cornwall spend their summers, was bought at the same time as Balmoral. Prince Albert set about making improvements to the woodlands, gardens and estate buildings, and commissioned the City Architect of Aberdeen, William Smith, to design a new house altogether.

The old castle of Balmoral was demolished and the new castle, in the Scots Baronial style, was completed during 1856. Built of local pink granite, it comprises two main blocks, each arranged around a courtyard. The building is dominated on the south-east side by a 120-foot-high square clock tower topped with turrets where the Royal Standard flies when the Sovereign is in residence.

In her widowhood Queen Victoria found Balmoral a welcome retreat from "the world and its sad turmoils", spending up to four months there during summer and autumn. The castle was also a favourite with King George VI and the Queen Mother.

"A mere court butterfly, That flutters in the pageant of a monarch."
Lord Byron

The Royal Household

Queen Victoria's coronation procession on 28 June 1838. She is accompanied by her ladies-in-waiting who, she noted, were 'all dressed alike and beautifully in white satin and silver tissue with wreaths of silver corn-ears in front…'. Until Queen Victoria ascended the throne the female portion of the Royal Household was appointed by the political party in power. When Victoria was crowned she surrounded herself with her girlhood friends and refused to part with them. Know as the 'Bedchamber Question' the dispute kept Robert Peel out of office for two and a half years, as both sides refused to compromise.

A ROYAL HOUSEHOLD is a vital part of royal life. All members of the royal family who undertake public engagements have households of their own comprising the full-time members of their private offices and others who may from time to time be called upon to assist with their public duties. Each Royal Household works as a separate entity, although efforts are made to co-ordinate one with another.

The Royal Households of today are efficient organisations that give value for money; but a description of the various departments and offices within the Queen's Household just 50 years ago will evoke a sense of the history that Catherine will be walking into: The Department of the Keeper of the Privy Purse and Treasurer to the Queen, The Privy Purse Office, The Treasurer's Office, The Royal Almonry Office, The Lord Chamberlain's Office (including four 'Examiners of Plays' — theatre censorship was not abolished until 1968), along with 68 other named officials, The Ecclesiastical Household (plus 36 Chaplains), The Medical Household, The Marshal of the Diplomatic Corps, The Central Chancery of the Orders of Knighthood, The Master of the Household's Department, and The Royal Mews Department.

Equerry originates from the French word 'écuri' (stable), and relates to the French word 'écuyer' (squire). Historically, he was a senior attendant with responsibilities for the horses of a person of rank. In contemporary use, he is a personal attendant, usually upon a sovereign, or a senior member of a royal family. In Britain equerries are drawn only from senior officers of the British armed forces. For some years the Queen's senior equerry has also held the position of Deputy Master of the Household. Senior members of the British royal family each also have one or two equerries.

Ladies-in-waiting are responsible for looking after flowers, cards and presents, and helping with private correspondence. Originally, ladies-in-waiting were members of the nobility themselves, although this is no longer necessarily required. The role of a lady-in-waiting has also evolved; most modern ladies-in-waiting are discreet companions rather than simply members of a huge court entourage designed to impress and advertise the monarch's power.

Top: The Queen and Prince Philip arrive at the State Opening of Parliament in 1999, accompanied by the Queen's ladies-in-waiting The Duchess of Grafton (left) and Lady Farnham. Chosen from among friends of the royal family and senior courtiers for their loyalty and discretion, ladies-in-waiting must not be afraid to offer honest or useful advice.

Above: John Lavery, Equerry to the Prince of Wales, holding flowers given to the Prince during a walkabout in Romania in 1999. Equerries are no longer merely responsible for the King's horses. They are now seen as general attendants and may find themselves performing the equivalent duty to a lady-in-waiting for male members of the royal family.

"The couple are completely over the moon, I've never seen two happier people. It's fabulous to work in that sort of environment."
Jamie Lowther-Pinkerton,
Prince William's private secretary

A Modern Royal Household

UNTIL VERY RECENTLY the named members of royal households were still very extensive. Even in 1990 the Household of the Prince and Princess of Wales consisted of an equerry and a temporary equerry to the prince, five ladies-in-waiting and one extra lady-in-waiting to the princess, a private secretary (and treasurer), a deputy private secretary and two assistant private secretaries to the prince, a private secretary to the princess, and an apothecary to the Household, amounting to some 14 appointments. Obviously there would also have been large clerical and service staff to support the offices, and a large domestic staff to support the Household.

At present the Duke of Cambridge shares a Royal Household with his brother Prince Harry at Clarence House, which is also the official residence of their father, the Prince of Wales, and his wife, the Duchess of Cornwall. Prince William and Prince Harry also share the services of a private secretary, who has been with them since 2005, James Lowther-Pinkerton. He works at St. James's Palace.

For the time being, the Duke and Duchess of Cambridge have chosen to live a comparatively modest existence by royal standards, and certainly compared to the Household of the Prince of Wales. They are moving temporarily to an apartment in Kensington Palace and are keeping their house in Anglesey, close to the RAF base where William serves, as their main home. There have been no appointments of ladies-in waiting or equerries and they are resolved to manage with their super-efficient current staff of James Lowther-Pinkerton, Christopher Kealey (assistant private secretary), Miguel Head (press secretary), Sir David Manning (diplomatic advisor, sometime Ambassador to the USA), Thea Garwood (Prince William's engagement secretary) and Helen Asprey (personal assistant). Their tour of Canada and California in June/July 201 was a test-run of this new, streamlined household.

Inevitably, as Duke and Duchess of Cambridge, they will eventually be given a separate royal residence by the Queen and ultimately a separate Royal Household will probably also be required to support the young couple. William and Catherine's wedding has blended traditional and modern features. A well-chosen Royal Household, which reflects both the old and the new, will enable them to enjoy their lives both as members of one the most famous families in the world, and as private individuals.

Left: The Duke and Duchess of Cambridge meet President Obama and Michelle Obama during their State Visit to Britain on 24 May 2011. On state occasions, the Duke and Duchess are advised by Sir David Manning, an experienced diplomat, whom the Queen appointed as a mentor to Prince William in 2010 when he was about to make his first tour of Australia and New Zealand. In the run-up to the wedding Sir David guided Catherine Middleton on royal protocol and foreign affairs. In the 1940s, when her father was still on the throne, the Queen had a similar advisory relationship with the decorated war hero General Sir Frederick 'Boy' Browning.

Above left: Prince William attends the opening of the 21st World Scout Jamboree in 2007 under the watchful eye of his Private Secretary Jamie Lowther-Pinkerton. The former SAS soldier, who also served as an equerry to the Queen Mother, has been Prince William's and Prince Harry's private secretary since 2005.

Above right: Jamie Lowther-Pinkerton steps in to what is usually a lady-in-waiting's role when he takes flowers from Catherine Middleton during a walkabout after she attended the Naming Ceremony and Service of Dedication of the Atlantic 85 Lifeboat at Trearddur Bay, Anglesey, on 24 February 2011.

"Now I can look the East End in the face."
Queen Elizabeth, the Queen Mother

Meeting the Public

A CRUCIAL ELEMENT OF kingship is being visible to the people. Queen Elizabeth I, mindful of the disastrous reigns of her two predecessors, Queen Mary Tudor and Lady Jane Grey, was acutely aware of the importance of the relationship between Monarch and People. She went on 'progresses' throughout the country, with her Court, to stay with various noblemen. Richly attired and attended, she was the very image of a loving Sovereign in touch with her people.

Three hundred years later Queen Victoria, in her long years of widowhood, lost much of her popularity by shutting herself away in Windsor Castle, leading *The Times* to write that 'the living have their claims as well as the dead'. Eventually public opinion forced the Queen to return to London, and celebrations of her golden and diamond jubilees (*above*) did much to restore her prestige in the public eye.

Queen Victoria's son and successor, King Edward VII, was the first monarch of the modern age to appreciate and exploit the charismatic effect of pageantry and royal ceremonial. On his accession he immediately broke with precedent by personally opening the new session of parliament on 14 February 1901 and reading the speech from the throne.

In the reign of Queen Victoria's grandson, the Delhi Durbar (a Persian word for 'Court') of December 1911 was held to crown the newly-enthroned King George V and Queen Mary as Emperor and Empress of India. They were the only British monarchs to visit India during the period of British rule, and the only British monarchs to attend the Durbar in person.

King George VI and Queen Elizabeth were evidently also aware of the impact that personal contact could make on the public; in May 1939 a CBC commentator covering the King and Queen's unveiling of the National War Memorial in Ottawa, Canada, noted that the smiling royal couple unexpectedly plunged into a throng of Great War veterans, shook hands and chatted with thrilled old soldiers – this was an early example of an impromptu 'walkabout'.

During the war years, the frequent patriotic broadcasts of King George VI were celebrated for their impact on public morale. His wife famously possessed 'the common touch' and endeared herself most appealingly to the country when, on being urged to seek safety with her daughters by evacuating to Canada or the USA, said "the children won't go without me. I won't leave the King. And the King will never leave".

King George V and Queen Mary went to the Delhi Durbar of 1911 to be crowned as Emperor and Empress of India, the only British monarchs to ever set foot in the subcontinent. Dressed in their Coronation robes, the King-Emperor wore the Imperial Crown of India, containing 6,170 exquisitely cut diamonds, and covered with sapphires, emeralds and rubies. They witnessed an event of unprecedented pomp in Indian history. Every ruling prince, nobleman and official attended the ceremonies, including a dazzling parade of elephants, to pay homage to their Sovereigns. Over half a million people turned out to greet them when they appeared at a balcony of the Red Fort. A feature film of the coronation titled *With Our King and Queen Through India* (1912) – also known as *The Durbar in Delhi* – was filmed in the early colour process Kinemacolor and released on 2 February 1912.

King George VI and Queen Elizabeth stand in the rubble of a bombed-out London street on 8 October 1940. Their resolve to stay in London during the Blitz was widely admired, and their frequent contact with Londoners during the War was a great boost to civilian morale.

"So much of this visit reminds us of the complexity of our history; its many layers and traditions, but also the importance of forbearance and conciliation. Of being able to bow to the past, but not be bound by it."
Queen Elizabeth II, State Visit to Ireland 2011

Walkabouts and State Visits

ROYALTY BECAME INSTANTLY MORE ACCESSIBLE with the advent of the 'walkabout'. When the Queen and the Duke of Edinburgh visited New Zealand in March 1970 they took the crowds by surprise when they left their official car and walked some 400 yards along the street, stopping to greet and speak to some of the many thousands who had waited patiently for the royal couple. Since then the royal walkabout has become an essential part of most provincial and overseas visits, often providing wonderful photo opportunities, and giving the royal family an attractively open image.

The Sovereign is perhaps most visible of all on a State Visit. The Queen has made nearly 110 State Visits since her accession to the throne in 1952, and the Duke of Edinburgh has invariably been by her side. A State Visit is the highest form of diplomatic contact between nations, and a visit by the Queen, who is the head of 16 countries, draws much publicity, media attention and large crowds.

Today there are usually two or three incoming State Visits a year. They are celebrated with a great deal of pomp and circumstance – including a private luncheon with the Queen, a carriage drive through the heart of 'ceremonial' London, a State banquet, a reception with high commissioners and ambassadors, a banquet at Guildhall as the guest of the Lord Mayor of London and a visit to Downing Street.

Official visits from newly-wed royal couples are eagerly anticipated. Very soon after their marriage had made headlines all over the world, the Prince and Princess of Wales made their first official visit together, a three-day tour of Wales. In 1982 Princess Diana undertook her first official visit solo, when she represented the Queen at the state funeral of Princess Grace of Monaco.

In March 2011 her son Prince William visited New Zealand and Australia, where he paid special attention to those who had suffered in recent natural disasters and to the volunteers who had dealt with the aftermath. Before the wedding, Catherine Middleton was gently 'eased in' to the royal role, when she accompanied Prince William on a number of occasions: she launched a new lifeboat in Anglesey, the couple visited their old university, St. Andrews, she flipped pancakes in Belfast and visited an academy and country park in Blackburn, Lancashire. in Blackburn, Lancashire. Their first overseas tour, to Canada and California, took place in June/July 2011.

Far left: Queen Elizabeth II riding an elephant in Benares during a tour of India, 25 January 1961. Elizabeth and Prince Philip received a rapturous welcome in southern India, with State governments declaring holidays in Chennai and Bangalore. "Hundreds of thousands of people," *The Hindu* of 20 February 1961 reported, "lined the nineteen-mile route from the Meenambakkam airport to the heart of Madras, to give an unprecedented welcome to Queen Elizabeth and the Duke of Edinburgh."

Left: Protocol on overseas visits is taken care of by the Foreign and Commonwealth Office and the Diplomatic Corps. For example when Prince William visited New Zealand in March 2011 he met Maori elder Mary Tulloch, and performed the traditional greeting (rubbing noses), known as *hongi*.

Catherine Middleton talks with children during a walkabout after attending a naming ceremony and service of dedication for a new lifeboat 'Hereford Endeavour' at Trearddur Bay, Anglesey on 24 February 2011. This was the couple's first official engagement. The Prince told the crowd "I do the talking, she does the fun bit" before Catherine Middleton poured champagne over the boat. She impressed the crowds by singing the Welsh national anthem.

"I hope by deepening my understanding of the issue I can help do my bit to help the most vulnerable on our streets."
Prince William

The Royal Family and Patronage

THE PRACTICE OF THE PATRONAGE of societies, organisations and charities by the royal family has been an integral feature of royal life since at least the reign of King George III.

The Prince of Wales alone is (or has been) patron or president of nearly 400 organisations, and is constantly hosting receptions, dinners and meetings on their behalf. The value of having a member of the royal family as a patron or president cannot be overstated. It guarantees an interest by the local press and, sometimes, by the national press and television networks. The Sovereign's name is of course the most prized on any list of patrons, and the Queen has been able to undertake some sort of engagement for most of the 800 or so organisations on her list.

The late Diana, Princess of Wales, was a most effective patron of Centrepoint, the charity that supports young homeless people, until her death in 1997, and the charity now enjoys the patronage of Prince William, who accepted the role in 2005. It is not a commitment to be taken lightly. On 22 December 2009 Prince William (together with his private secretary Jamie Lowther-Pinkerton and the chief-executive of Centrepoint, Seyi Obakin) made their way into

central London, around Blackfriars Bridge, to spend the night sleeping rough, at a temperature that fell as low as -4°C (*above*). The press coverage was unprecedented.

Applications for the patronage of any member of the royal family are submitted to the appropriate private secretary. Careful enquiries into the integrity of the charity are carried out, and ministerial advice might be sought before patronage is granted. It is unusual for more than one member of the royal family to accept a patronage of a single charity, but this has happened with Princes William and Harry who are joint-patrons of The Henry van Straubenzee Memorial Fund.

Most members of the royal family take the view that it is best to limit their patronage to the organisations in which they have a genuine interest and which they can actively support. William and Catherine took the unusual step of using their wedding as a means of promoting their favourite charities, many of which are without a royal patron, by inaugurating a Charitable Gift Fund for the Royal Wedding. Their list focused on charities that promote the welfare of disadvantaged young people and returning servicemen as well as conservation work, and raised a total of £1,058,367.

William, an Aston Villa fan, became President of the Football Association in 2006. In 2010 he joined David Cameron and David Beckham in an English bid to host the 2018 World Cup. He is seen here in 2007 at a Hat-trick project at West Gate Community College Centre for Sport in Newcastle where young people from the charity Centrepoint, of which he is also patron, were taking part in a football course.

As Diana grew in confidence she became more and more committed to charities concerned with children, the disabled and AIDS victims, and she became increasingly adept at using the media to raise their profiles in the public eye. She will always be remembered for her tireless work against landmines. Following a visit to Angola in January 1997, the Princess caused controversy when she called for an international ban on landmines.

*After first addressing the Queen as 'Your Majesty'
the subsequent form of address is "Ma'am" to
rhyme with jam. Members of the royal family
who are HRH are first addressed as "Your Royal
Highness", and subsequently as "Sir" or "Ma'am".*

Royal Protocol

IN AUGUST 2009 A STORY went round the national press that
the time-honoured tradition of walking backwards upon
taking leave of the Sovereign was to be done away with.
It was reported that officials at Buckingham Palace were
concerned that a visitor leaving the royal presence might
accidentally stumble and fall. Ever the pragmatist, it is highly
unlikely that the Queen made the mildest objection to this
departure from tradition.

However, the Marshal of the Diplomatic Corps, a senior
member of the Royal Household, is still expected to
maintain the old standards. He is the link between the
Sovereign and the foreign diplomatic missions, responsible
for collecting ambassadors and high commissioners from their
residences and taking them by state landau to Buckingham
Palace, where they present their credentials to the Queen
whilst the Marshal, walking backwards, discreetly withdraws.

Two other senior members of the Royal Household were
(until 2003) required by tradition to walk backwards before
the Queen at the State Opening of Parliament. These were
the Earl Marshal (the Duke of Norfolk) and the Lord Great
Chamberlain (the Marquess of Cholmondeley), both of

whom are Great Officers of State. Jack Straw (when Lord Chancellor) re-instituted the tradition of walking backwards down the steps of the throne after presenting the Speech to the Queen, but in 2010, at the Earl Marshal's suggestion, the Lord Chancellor (Kenneth Clarke) did not do so.

Upon presentation to the Queen, or to any other member of the royal family bearing the qualification HRH, it is traditional to bow or curtsey. A man should bow just from the neck, and a woman should make a short curtsey or 'bob'. Although Buckingham Palace has in recent years taken the line that it is a question of personal preference whether or not to make the traditional bow or curtsey to the Queen and to other members of the royal family, it is still to be strongly recommended that the senior members of the royal family should be given these forms of respect.

The dress code for royal events is made clear on the invitation – usually issued by the Master of the Household – whether for a royal wedding, a garden party, or investiture.

A 2003 memo from the British Consulate General sensibly advised its staff prior to a visit by the Princess Royal that "it is customary to wait for the member of the royal family to extend a hand, initiate a topic of conversation, etc, but there is no need to worry; just be yourself."

The tradition of not touching the Queen (always excepting a gentle handshake) is well known, and indeed for most people a handshake is generally considered sufficient physical contact upon a first meeting with any total stranger. When the unfortunate Prime Minister of Australia, Paul Keating, was seen to put his arm around the Queen's waist at Canberra's Parliament House in 1992, the British press were vocal in their criticism of his temerity.

The younger princes and princesses, including the Duke and Duchess of Cambridge, may very well neither wish for, nor expect, displays of deference, except perhaps on a formal introduction. If there is any doubt about protocol it might be safer to make enquiries to the private secretary before the circumstances arise.

Left: Queen Elizabeth II receives the Ambassador of Italy Mr Alain Giorgio Maria Economides at Buckingham Palace where he formally presents his diplomatic credentials.

Above: There was very great interest when, at the visit of President and Mrs Obama to Buckingham Palace at the G20 reception on 1 April 2009, the Queen was noted to lightly touch the small of Mrs Obama's back as the two made conversation. Mrs Obama responded with a friendly arm almost across the Queen's shoulder. It was certainly an unusually tactile moment, but charmingly informal, and a pleasant relaxation of the usual protocol at such an event. In the words of President Obama, "It was a wonderful visit…Her Majesty is delightful."

At 8am on Friday 29 April 2011, the day of the royal wedding, Buckingham Palace released a statement to say that The Queen had created her grandson, Prince William of Wales, Duke of Cambridge. The title does not bring any mansion or land with it, but it is a historic title, imbued with prestige, learning and romance, which will admirably suit the young prince and princess.

The Duke and Duchess of Cambridge

George III created his 7th son, HRH Prince Adolphus, Duke of Cambridge in 1801. He was a Lieutenant General in the British Army and (appropriately) Chancellor of St. Andrews University. He was the grandfather of Princess May of Teck (Queen Mary).

HRH Prince George, 2nd Duke of Cambridge, was Commander-in-Chief of the British Forces 1856–95. He married an actress, Louisa Fairbrother, who was known as 'Mrs FitzGeorge' and ignored by the Queen (the descendants are named FitzGeorge-Balfour).

THE CORRECT FORMS OF ADDRESS for William and Catherine are now His Royal Highness The Duke of Cambridge, and Her Royal Highness The Duchess of Cambridge. Like all dukedoms (both royal and non-royal) the title also has lesser (or subsidiary) titles, in this case Earl of Strathearn and Baron Carrickfergus, but in all official publications, including the Court Circular, they will simply be known as the Duke and Duchess of Cambridge.

In conferring a dukedom upon her grandson, the Queen was conforming to a long-observed royal tradition. The first royal dukes were created on the same day in 1362, when King Edward III created his third son, Lionel of Antwerp, Duke of Clarence, and his fourth son, John of Gaunt, Duke of Lancaster. He further created his fifth son, Edmund of Langley, Duke of York, and his youngest son, Thomas of Woodstock, Duke of Gloucester, on the same day in 1385.

Closer to the present day, the Queen created her second son, Prince Andrew, Duke of York on his wedding day in 1986, and also created her youngest son, Prince Edward, Earl of Wessex upon his wedding day in 1999. Upon the death of the present Duke of Edinburgh the dukedom will descend to the Prince of

Prince William received his Coat of Arms on his 18th birthday, in 2000. The design is derived from the armorial bearings of the Queen, but incorporates the red 'escallop' (sea-shell) from the arms of the Spencers.

Wales – and upon the Prince of Wales's succession to the throne Prince Edward will be created Duke of Edinburgh.

The Edmund of Langley already mentioned above was created Earl of Cambridge in 1362 (prior to being raised to Duke of York). This is the first time that Cambridge was used as a royal title. His second son, Richard of York, succeeded his father as Earl of Cambridge in 1402, and was beheaded on Southampton Green in 1415. Richard's grandson, King Edward IV, was Duke of York and Earl of Cambridge, but these titles merged with the Crown when he succeeded to the throne in 1461.

In the Stuart dynasty four sons of James, Duke of York (later King James II) were all created Duke of Cambridge, and all died in infancy. In the House of Hanover King George III created his 7th son, HRH Prince Adolphus, Duke of Cambridge in 1801. He was Lieutenant General in the British Army and Chancellor of St. Andrews University, and died in 1850, when he was succeeded by his son, HRH Prince George, 2nd Duke of Cambridge. He married in contravention of the Royal Marriages Act and the title became extinct upon his death in 1904. Cambridge later existed as a Marquessate from 1917, when it was conferred upon Queen Mary's brother, until 1981 when the 2nd Marquess died and the title again merged with the Crown.

CATHERINE MIDDLETON'S COAT OF ARMS

The College of Arms, situated in Queen Victoria Street, near St. Paul's, is part of the Queen's Household and is under the authority of the Earl Marshal (one of the Great Officers of State).

Applications for a Coat of Arms are first submitted to the Earl Marshal (the Duke of Norfolk), who authorises every new grant of arms by issuing a warrant to one or more of the three senior heralds: Garter King of Arms, Clarenceux King of Arms, and Norroy and Ulster King of Arms. One of the Kings of Arms or one of the other heralds is responsible for the design of the Coat of Arms.

It is usual for the wife of a royal prince to have her own arms, and it is no surprise that Catherine's father, Michael Middleton, wished to apply for a grant for his family. The design released by the College of Arms was approved and agreed by Thomas Woodcock, Garter King of Arms, in consultation with the Middleton family.

Catherine Middleton's Coat of Arms is presented on a 'lozenge' rather than on a shield, in deference to the female sex not generally being of a warlike disposition. In layman's terms the lozenge is divided vertically with one half blue and the other half red, crossed by a gold chevron (an inverted 'V' shape), with white lines on either side of the chevron, and three representations of a gold acorn on a leaved sprig, two above the chevron and one below.

The technical heraldic description (known as a blazon) is: Per pale azure and gules a chevron or cotised argent between three acorns slipped and leaved or.

After her marriage, Catherine Middleton will place her father's arms beside those of Prince William in an 'impaled' Coat of Arms. This will require a Royal Warrant from the Queen.

The Legacy

Royalists had predicted a glorious day, but the impact of the wedding far exceeded expectations. April saw Great Britain suddenly bloom in red, white and blue, while bunting spread like spring tendrils. Images of William and Kate beamed from mugs, posters, tea towels and books. A long winter of economic gloom had finally given way to jubilation and the public, preparing for a nationwide party, were ready to embrace their future King and Queen.

"We're quite a reserved lot, the British, but when we go for it, we really go for it."
David Cameron

The Impact of the Day

"IT WAS EXCELLENT," said Her Majesty Queen Elizabeth II of her grandson's wedding, and the world agreed with her verdict. The great institutions of Monarchy, Church, Government and the Military had swung into action to stage a pageant of solemnity and splendour.

The pride of Britain's armed forces gave a thrilling display (in an Austen-esque moment it was revealed that Nicholas van Cutsem, who commanded the Captain's Escort of Household Cavalry, would ride a charger called Darcy). The most accomplished musicians performed stirring British anthems. The finest of the nation's craftsmanship was showcased in the bride's apparel and its best produce was used to create dishes for both receptions. A Forest of Arden was created in Westminster Abbey, which was decked out with towering English maples and hornbeams. A great British motorcar, an Aston Martin DB6 Volante, took the couple away to Clarence House.

Yet, at the heart of all that spectacle and formality, there was spontaneity and joy. It was easy to discern the delight and ease between the royal groom and his bride, signalling a union of equals.

In the build-up to the day, however, some were sceptical of its impact and the likely turnout. In the 30 years since Prince Charles married Lady Diana Spencer there had been a slow erosion of royal mystique: the public's romance with the monarchy had been undermined by unseemly revelations and the fallout from Diana's death. Meanwhile a new generation, born since the last marriage of an heir to the throne, were untutored in the art of flag-waving. Four years of economic crisis and a winter of public sector cuts had sapped the nation's optimism and bravado. While many Americans showed unabashed fervour for this fairy-tale romance, Britons tended to be on a slower burn – so slow at times some feared the fuse had gone out.

William and Catherine were sensitive to the country's mood. They knew shows of bombast would prove unpopular in Austerity Britain, nor was it their style. Diana's determination that her son should live as "ordinary" a life as possible, under the most singular circumstances, had borne fruit. He had chosen a girl from a refreshingly functional middle-class background and the pair were busy staging their own small velvet revolution, overturning a charabanc of royal protocol. Cars, not

Far left: A commemorative plate from the range commissioned and designed by The Royal Collection (which was created to curate the royal family's huge collection of priceless art and artefacts). This is the only china that has an official seal of approval from the Royal Household. The wedding range included three pieces: a tankard, plate and pillbox. As is traditional, the items were handcrafted in the potteries of Stoke-on-Trent using methods unchanged for 250 years.

Left: Traditional British confectioners Swizzels Matlow produced a limited edition of their famous Love Heart sweeties to commemorate the royal wedding, with the words 'Just Married' on each sweet. Manchester artist Mark Kennedy was commissioned by the firm to create a mural of the royal couple's faces entirely from Love Hearts and the artwork went on display in the City's Spinningfields district as the centrepiece of its street party.

Left: The royal family do not sanction the use of their faces on official china, so collectors wanting portraits of the couple had to look to other ranges. Less stately commemorative products also proved popular, including royal biscuits (pictured), tea, peppermints and even a celebratory London Transport Oyster Card.

"We've really got to know Kate. She is really caring. She is like a human being, not a celebrity, and she is always a good customer. William is very down to earth."
Chan and Hash Shingadia, who run the Middletons' local store in Bucklebury

carriages, would be used to transport the royal wedding party to the Abbey, while the military's involvement would not place undue strains upon their capacity. Prince William's private secretary issued a statement saying: "… the couple are very mindful of the current situation and, for example, Prince William has already expressed a clear wish that any involvement by the armed forces should rely in great part on those servicemen and women already committed to public and ceremonial duties."

William and Catherine became the first royal couple to dispense with a wedding list, asking instead that donations be made to select charities. Catherine posed for her engagement photo in a high street dress (she left Buckingham Palace, after the wedding, in a Zara frock that cost £49.99). This was a girl who styled her hair simply and did her own make-up, even on her wedding day with two billion viewers scrutinising her. She let it be known that she would not be appointing any ladies-in-waiting. Prince William prioritised his forces' colleagues in the invitations, asking a number to the wedding breakfast, alongside executives of his favourite charities, leaving some high profile celebrities to forage for themselves after the service.

The couple's lack of pretension charmed the public. In the fortnight before the nuptials, the British people stirred like a slumbering behemoth waking from a long dream. A quarter of the nation's street parties were registered in the fortnight preceding the wedding and suddenly the bunting, flags and celebratory china began to sell. Families began to talk of going to London for the big day so their children could witness a slice of history. Many who had expressed a lack of interest began to quietly plot TV parties with their friends and neighbours.

Unlikely best sellers showed the country was finally in celebratory mood. A book entitled *Knit Your Own Royal Wedding*, with instructions for creating your own woollen balcony scene, sold like hot cakes. Royal gnomes proved popular, as did swishy-locked Kate dolls. Sainsbury's supermarkets stocked its own unique T-shirt with the caption: "Kate and William sitting in a tree K.I.S.S.I.N.G." Other popular slogans included: "Thank you for the day off" and "It should have been me". Replica sapphire and diamond engagement rings sold all round the world and the *Sun* newspaper offered free imitations in exchange for tokens. The singer George Michael recorded a cover version of

London's gift stalls were bursting with commemorative products including tea-towels, which have long been a staple of the wedding memorabilia trade. In December 2010 it was widely reported that the Lord Chamberlain had issued a ban on cloths carrying images of Prince William and Catherine Middleton. A spokesman for Buckingham Palace said, "We want items that are permanent and significant." In the event The Royal Collection issued its own irreproachably tasteful tea towel in Clarence House blue, with the couple's entwined initials, but no photographs. Meanwhile the Lord Chamberlain relented and the time-honoured trade in mug-shot towels continued unabated. After china and tea-towels, the third most popular celebratory item was The Royal Mint coin, which sold for £5.00 and was approved by the couple.

Three days after the Royal Wedding copies of Catherine Middleton's gown had already flooded the market. In New York's Faviana fashion house two versions of the 'Princess Kate' dress were on display: the more expensive and faithful replica is to the left, while a cheaper version, with a less regal skirt, is to the right.

"I don't think brides will want an exact replica. The train is too long for most brides. We are making it shorter, so that brides can bustle the gown and dance the night away."
Shala Morada, chief designer, Faviana

Stevie Wonder's hit "You and I" as a free download to honour the son of his friend Diana and maintained it wasn't a hint he should be asked to the wedding. There were Royal Wedding nail decorations and tooth transfers, and even a celebratory London Transport Oyster Card. One infamous mug manufactured by Guandong Enterprises, sported the message, "The fairytale romantic union of all the centuries" alongside photos of a beaming Catherine and Prince Harry.

Despite the building excitement, figures released by PricewaterhouseCoopers on the eve of the wedding wildly underestimated the turnout. The accountants were gauging the event's economic impact with figures based on a crowd of half a million lining the wedding route. In the event, twice that number stood and cheered, while tens of thousands partied in Trafalgar Square and St. James's Park; an impressive 100,000 revellers turned up to watch the service on the big screen at Hyde Park. So the firm's estimate that visitor spending would benefit the capital to the tune of £107 million was far short of the mark. The long-term benefits of the royal wedding were put at a £2 billion boost to the British economy over the following year. 'Brand Kate' alone was said by some to be worth more to Britain than the Olympics. According to one

survey, the average spend on celebratory items was £23. The total sale of royal merchandise was expected to top £40 million. All this put gripes about the wedding costs – around £20 million – into sharp perspective.

Yet the greatest boost of all was to the national psyche. The banking crisis and scandal surrounding politicians' expenses had sapped the country's confidence in its institutions. On Prince William's wedding day the public was reminded that Britain could still pull together in spectacular fashion and astound the world. The atmosphere in London on 29th April was electrifying. On the night before the wedding Central London's streets had been eerily calm, but from first light the people flooded back into the capital, bearing flags and periscopes aloft.

In front of Westminster Abbey at 7am a little girl called Stephanie drew smiles with her long white satin gown, tiara and sceptre, and her yearning to be a princess. Amongst the crowds on Whitehall at 9am stood a handsome young Brazilian with a glitter-paint Union flag precision-executed on his face; his group of friends included visitors from Korea, Japan, France and Germany.

The day after the royal wedding Vanessa Kelterborn, a manager at ABS Clothing Collection Inc in Santa Monica, California, arranges a replica of Catherine's gown in the store's window. As soon as the bride stepped out before the world's media, designers were sketching her dress and the race was on to make the swiftest imitation. The fastest British imitation was created by designer Mary-Rose McGrath and went on display in Belfast's House of Fraser store within 24 hours of the wedding service. In China a polyester version of the dress was also available within a day of the wedding, selling for $333.

A team of Australian designers accepted the challenge laid down by *Woman's Day* magazine to complete faithful replicas of both the bride's and maid of honour's dresses over one weekend, following the royal wedding. The team started at 10pm on Friday night and finished on Sunday lunchtime. Designer Karen Willis Holmes who copied Kate's dress said she felt it was, "80 to 90 per cent close to the original design." Meanwhile a team of pastry chefs baked an imitation six-tiered wedding cake. The completed finery was on display at Sydney's Queen Victoria Building by 2 May 2011.

*"I think they are deeply unpretentious people...
They've had a very simple, very direct picture of
what really matters about this event."*
The Archbishop of Canterbury

At 11am in St. James's Park, the Women's Institute of Nercwys proclaimed Wales's love of the Royals, while singing Cwm Rhondda. A young man wearing a horse's head wandered past, while another was dressed as a tiger. Many young women in wedding dresses sported replica rings, but one six-foot male student in a white gown attracted all the wolf-whistles. Later, in the jolly mayhem of the masses before Buckingham Palace's gates, people parted to give space to a sleek Hungarian Viszla wearing its very own Union flag. An amateur dramatics society from Somerset formed a group tableau as the royal family, with masks, costumes and a cardboard balcony.

When the royal family stepped out to greet the crowds one little girl spoke for the whole crowd when she gasped, "I saw the Queen – I saw all their faces." As the unmistakable hum of Merlin engines was heard to the east every head turned and hearts lifted as the Lancaster, flanked by a Spitfire and Hurricane, came into view, swooping low over the Palace in tribute to the newlyweds and to the country. A verger at Westminster Abbey was observed, when the building had emptied, turning a couple of exuberant cartwheels in the aisle, and everyone shared his sentiments.

In the following days Britain floated on a cloud of euphoria, suddenly aware that the world envied them their royal heritage. The goodwill towards the couple was further boosted when it was announced that Prince William was returning to work a few days after the wedding, just like the rest of the nation. Shortly after the couple arrived in Anglesey, Catherine (as the world was learning to call the Duchess) was photographed in jeans and a jumper pushing a shopping trolley into Waitrose. The gap between royalty and subjects had rarely been bridged so emphatically.

29 April 2011 was the day Britons were reminded how fortunate they are to have a non-political Head of State, who reigns but does not rule, and who is regarded with universal warmth and esteem. They also recognised how lucky they were to have, in the person of her dashing grandson, a fitting heir. Always at the heart of celebrations was the young RAF helicopter pilot, who had shown fortitude at his mother's death, courage in his career, and immense wisdom in his choice of bride – for Catherine Wales captivates everyone she meets. On Prince William's wedding day Great Britain took the monarchy, reinvented for the modern age, back to its heart.

A chic Princess Catherine doll by Arklu went on sale in Harrods in April. The suitably sylph-like doll wore a replica of the iconic blue Issa frock that Catherine wore for her engagement interview with Tom Bradby and came with a jaunty set of accessories including gold shoes, a pink fascinator and a duplicate of the bride's Eaton clutch bag. The doll's ring even contained a real amethyst – if not the huge sapphire of the original. Arklu's director, Lucie Follett, said, "What we're doing here is promoting British designers and putting them out there, and saying, hey, it's all about British style."

A group of students from the Royal College of Art pose for photos outside Buckingham Palace, wearing imitations of Catherine's famous Issa dress and replicas of her engagement ring. The British fondness for fancy dress came to the fore with news of the royal wedding and on 29th April London's streets were adorned with young women in bridal gowns, princess dresses and faux jewels. Some even turned looking like Kate into a profession; in November 2010 a brunette from Stafford, Kate Bevan, gave up her job as a pharmaceutical assistant to become a full-time Catherine lookalike, after she was repeatedly stopped by people mistaking her for the bride. She even took elocution lessons in an attempt to lose her West Midlands' accent.

"Let love be genuine; hate what is evil, hold fast to what is good; love one another with mutual affection; outdo one another in showing honour…"
Romans 12, read at the marriage ceremony of Prince William and Catherine Middleton

Index

Acknowledgments

Getty Images: 6/7, 8, 12btm, 13, 18btm, 19, 24, 29, 33l, 33r, 35l, 40, 42 top, 44top, 47top r, 47mid l, 47mid r, 47btm, 48l, 50btm, 63btm, 69, 70, 73l, 74, 75top, 75btm, 82l, 83, 85, 86, 88, 89, 92, 95, 97, 98, 101top, 101btm, 106, 109, 110 top, 110btm, 111, 112, 113, 114, 115r, 119, 120, 121r, 123, 125, 126, 131, 135l, 135r, 137top l, 137top r, 137mid l, 137btm l, 137btm r, 139top r, 142l, 149l, 149btm, 150, 151top, 151btm, 152, 153 top, 153btm, 156top, 164, 167

© **Mary Evans Picture Library/Alamy:** 10, 11, 158l, 158r

The Granger Collection/ Topfoto/TopFoto.co.uk/: 14top

AFP/Getty Images: 14btm, 37top, 44btm, 52top, 53middle, 68, 91top, 91btm, 93, 96, 99, 102, 103, 108, 116, 117, 118, 121l, 130, 132, 133, 139top l, 139mid l, 139mid r, 139mid l, 139btm l, 139btm r, 163top, 168

Bridgeman Art Library/ Getty Images: 18top

Popperfoto/Getty Images: 19, 52btm

© **The British Library Board (MS Roy EVI f.9v.):** 20

© **Philip Mould Ltd, London/Bridgeman Art Library:** 21top l

© **National Portrait Gallery, London:** 21top r, 21btm, 23l, 23r

Time & Life Pictures/Getty Images: 21mid

© **INTERFOTO/Alamy:** 22l

© **Chetham's Library, Manchester/Bridgeman Art Library:** 22r

The Royal Collection © 2011, Her Majesty Queen Elizabeth II/Bridgeman Art Library: 26

The Royal Collection © 2011, Her Majesty Queen Elizabeth II: 27, 43, 44, 55

© **Illustrated London News Ltd/Mary Evans:** 28, 31btm, 32, 34, 38, 50top

Print Collector/HIP/ Topfoto/TopFoto.co.uk: 30

© **Bettmann/Corbis:** 31top

Wire Image/Getty Images: 36, 72, 90, 104, 170-71

Press Association: 37btm, 46, 47top l, 53top, 56, 58, 62, 67mid, 94, 157,

Tim Graham/Getty Images: 39top, 48r, 67top, 67btm, 73 mid, 73r, 143btm, 147top, 147btm, 149l, 155top

TopFoto/UPP/topFoto. co.uk: 39btm

Ben Roberts/Clogau Gold: 42btm

Lichfield/Getty Images: 49, 57

© **Museum of London/HIP/ TopFoto.co.uk:** 51

© **Topham Picturepoint/ TopFoto.co.uk:** 53btm

Associated Newspapers/ Daily Mail/Rex Features: 54

The Stapleton Collection/ Bridgeman Art Library: 59l

© **Trinity Mirror/ Mirrorpix/Alamy:** 59r, 60

Mirrorpix: 61

TopFoto/TopFoto.co.uk: 63top

Daily Mail/Rex Features: 64

Photo by the Middleton Family/Clarence House via Getty Images: 71, 76, 78 79, 80

Rex Features: Stephen Lock 81, Tony Kyriacou, 82r,

© **Alamy Celebrity/Alamy:** 84

Film Magic/Getty Images: 100, 105

Hugo Burnard/St James's Palace/Getty Images: 128, 129top, 129btm

flickr Editorial/Getty Images: 137mid r

© **The Art Gallery Collection / Alamy:** 140

© **Angleo Hornak/Alamy:** 142

The Stapleton Collection/ Bridgeman Art Library: 143top

© **Simon Belcher/Alamy:** 144

© **Mark Boulton/Alamy:** 145top: 145top

SSPL via Getty Images: 143btm

© **The Trustees of the British Museum/**Department of Prints and Drawings (1893,0612.247): 146

Centrepoint/Rex Features: 154

Tim Ireland/PA Wire: 156btm

Clarence House/AP/Press Association Images: 159l

Suzanne Plunkett/PA Wire/ Press Association Images: 159r

Paul Grover/Daily Telegraph/PA Wire: 160

Royal Collection © 2010 HM Queen Elizabeth II/Rex Features: 162

Bloomberg via Getty Images: 163btm

Geoffrey Swaine/Rex Features: 165

AP Photo/Bebeto Matthews: 166

AP Photo/Jae C. Hong: 167top

Matt Dunham/AP/Press Association Images: 169

BELLYBAND

Back, **Getty Images;** spine, **AFP/Getty Images;** Front left, **Tim Graham/Getty Images;** Front remaining, **Getty Images**

Debrett's would like to thank Christopher Child, of the New England Historic Genealogical Society